T0372217

OLOID

OLOID

Form of the Future

Paul Schatz Foundation
Paul Schatz Society

CONTENTS

6   **Design off the beaten path**
Lucius Burckhardt

10   **Form based on motion**
Tobias Langscheid and Tilo Richter

14   **Unleashing the dance of life**
Dirk Böttcher

28   **About the crystals' "building and habitation"**
Paul Schatz

32   **The polysomatic sculpture**
On the foundation of new stereometric figures
Paul Schatz

40   **The oloid**
Origin and history
Matthias Mochner

48   **On the origin of the oloid, its geometry**
and phenomena
Felix M. Hediger

54   **Spatial variations: the cuboid oloid**
Christoph Müller

60   **"You have to invert your life!"**
Walter Kugler

68   **Panta rhei**
The oloid and water
Tobias Langscheid

76   **The oloid returns something to nature**
Gerhard Heid and Beate Oberdorfer

80   **Flying future concepts**
Inspiration based on inversion and the oloid
Heinrich Frontzek

84   **A comet in the art industry**
or: The UFO in the shop showcase
Andreas Chiquet

92   **Geometry and design**
Development of shape to oloid and inversion
Oliver Niewiadomski

108   **From form to space**
The oloid in architecture
Tilo Richter

120   **Performing Future**
The future principle is the principle of movement
Vera Koppehel

127   **Appendix**

Design off the beaten path

Lucius Burckhardt

1

Schatz investigates basic shapes, the five regular simple solids, which Euler proved to be the entire variety of solids. (Just a small reminder in passing of the non-Euclidean geometric shapes, which are not included here and that Andreas Speiser encourages architects and designers to study). Starting from the most familiar of the basic solids, the cube, Schatz came across a rather complicated phenomenon: a trisection into two outer solids and a belt that is invertible in a particular way. Schatz studied the surfaces that this cube belt moves along because of the inverting motion and saw that on these curves there is a particularly intense alternation of acceleration and deceleration in many different directions. Up to this point, he was led by his joy of discovery, venturing on obvious yet untraveled paths, and the beauty of the shapes. However, invention followed discovery: the movement performed by one of the edges of the invertible belt is nowadays used for mixing chemical substances. This motion moving along regular mathematical curves replaces the irrational shaking motion and produces, despite and because of its mathematical order, more perfect disorder in the substances to be mixed than all shaking and stirring. Even more, the movement of the inverted cube is so regular and yet so varied that it is used to automatically deburr and polish even the very tiniest components of a watch. When moved this way, the metallic parts rub against one another in a regular way and wear off the roughness of their edges. Is such an invention, made almost casually during an in-depth study of geometric bodies, not actually one of the greatest possibilities design can offer?

*First published in:
Das Werk: Architektur
und Kunst. Vol. 49 (1962),
H. 12 'Formgebung',
pp. 419–420*

left
Set of five platonic
solids in a design box,
all with the same
edge length, 1960s

below
Cube and cube seg-
ments — divided into
the cube belt and two
star bodies, 1960s

Design off the beaten path

The 48-part sphere
(or Kepler star) repre-
senting the 'stella
octangula', 1960s

Oloid

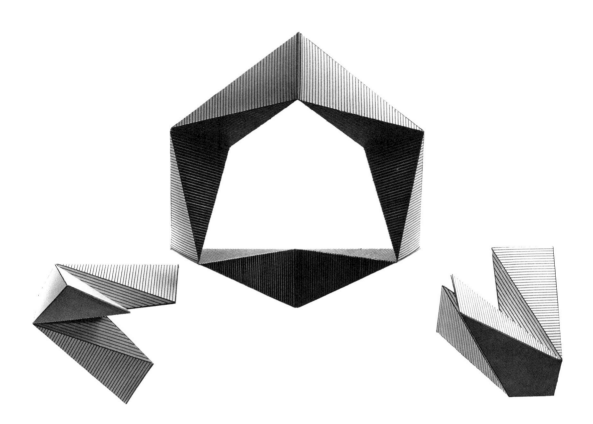

Star bodies and
cube belt of the inver-
tible cube, 1960s

Design off the beaten path

Form based on motion

Tobias Langscheid
Tilo Richter

2

In 1929, at the climax of Modernism, Paul Schatz discovered that the cube and all other regular solids are invertible. Following this, he also figured out that completely new shapes emerge from these fundamentally new laws of motion. The most striking amongst them is the oloid.

Schatz, a sculptor and researcher, rethought space and dissected geometric figures to set the resulting parts in motion. He derived previously unknown solids from kinetic sequences leaving three-dimensional traces in front of his eyes. Schatz's spatial sense beyond all existing norms coupled with his extraordinary perseverance in finding practical uses for the new shapes he created made him a pioneer of an entire era.

This first monograph on the oloid combines a variety of different aspects that developed and also partly influenced each other in the course of almost a century. Each time, the starting point is the rigid solid with its inverted movement in space that, in the case of the oloid, affects its environment in a completely new and surprising way: in water and in the air, as a light source or as an organically designed "worry stone"; as a source of inspiration for dance choreographies or musical compositions, as a perfect three-dimensional rhythm for mixing liquids, as encased space or as floating object reminiscent of zeppelins. Finally, the oloid gave and continues to give impulses for philosophical projections since it unites two fundamental aspects of time and thus of existence: point zero and infinity.

This book addresses all these different aspects and aims to satisfy the curiosity that this fascinating but inherently silent object wakens in many people. The purpose of our reflections is likewise to open new horizons for the oloid. Since its discovery, it has proven to be a universal body that – as simple as it is complex, and as elegant as it is powerful – has not yet revealed all its secrets and hidden potential.

Transparent epoxy resin oloid from the Paul Schatz Archive, around 1960

Form based on motion

Paul Schatz with a cube
belt, around 1970

Oloid

Model of a double–oloid
drive, Paul Schatz, 1930s

Form based on motion

Unleashing the dance of life

Dirk Böttcher

3

Paul Schatz turned the cube's interior inside out and thus came up with an unprecedented form: the oloid. It is the result of the universal recasting of an initial matter, the epitome of renewal – and thus more than ever an answer to urgent questions of our times.

What a metaphor! An inversion. Turning the innermost outward – resulting in an actual new composition of the original subject matter, a universal renewal. In physics this is called inversion. Such a fundamental process has rarely been as needed as much as it is today. Paul Schatz's philosophy, expressed in a concrete form in the oloid, provides an alternative approach to nature, to the way we live, think, handle our affairs, and consume. The oloid is a source of irritation for society and for each individual. It represents a movement both in the physical sense of the word as well as metaphorically. The oloid brakes and accelerates at the same time in a rhythmic pulsating motion by means of two pivot points.

Transforming a cube into a round object can change a lot of things in this world. After all, when giving things a new form, you discover that they take on other meanings and functions.

Today, the oloid, resulting from a cube's inversion, powers boats, converts wind power into electrical energy, mixes pharmaceutical substances, regenerates water and bodies of water, offers designers new strokes to use and thinkers new connections.

Technical explanations are one aspect, and certainly do not constitute the full picture – they may even be a false trail. The oloid is not at all something built. It was not created on the drawing board of an inventor, but through the effort of a sculptor, philosopher, mathematician, and visionary. Paul Schatz was all of this. At the age of seventeen already, he was driven by the idea of giving things a new look, of rethinking the world with these forms. As a teenager, he lived the insanity and dread of the First World War. He deeply longed for regeneration, as he tried to come to terms with what he experienced at the Western Front. After the war, Schatz believed that technology would bring about renewal.

He studied mathematics and mechanical engineering at the Technical University of Munich. Shortly before graduating he switched to astronomy. In 1922, he also abandoned this course of study, disappointed by the one-sided and abstract way of thinking in science. He then embarked on an artistic apprenticeship in Cieplice Śląskie-Zdrój in the Krkonoše Mountains, Poland, and made a living as a sculptor. In 1927, he moved with his partner Emmy Schatz-Witt to Dornach in Switzerland where he lived and worked as artist, inventor and technician.

It was the universal aspect of his work that broadened his view of things. Paul Schatz didn't create the oloid, he somehow came upon

Oloid light reflexes in the shape of a meander

Unleashing the dance of life

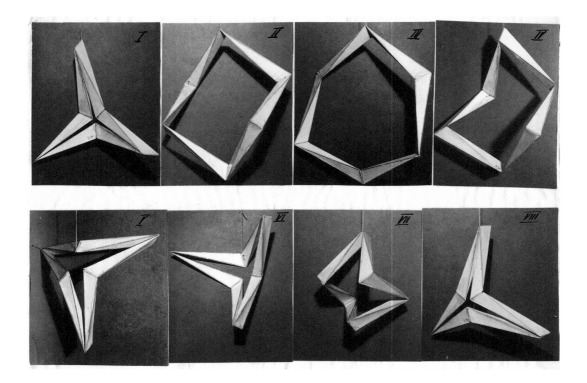

this unprecedented form. The path that led him to it was often contrary to the standard concepts of mathematics or technology, because the oloid is not a technical, but a spatial object. Born of and experienced in associative interaction with different disciplines, it still offers constantly new possibilities of interaction. Engineers are inspired by the oloid's shape for technical applications. Designers use it to redesign everyday objects, dancers follow the movement of the oloid in their choreographies.

Jumping into the deep end

Paul Schatz discovered the phenomenon of inversion, and through it the oloid shape in 1929. This was at his workshop in his Dornach home: 20 square meters crammed with wood and plaster models, immeasurable numbers of papers, and numerous peculiar measuring instruments. A magic realm. In the vicinity lies the so-called Blood Hill, where the Swiss Confederates defeated the imperial troops of the Swabian League in 1499 at the cost of a gruesome slaughter. For more than a century, this site has been home to the Goetheanum – the spiritual

top
Conversion movement
of the cuboid core prism
in eight steps, model of
the 1930s

right
Latest project: oloid fan
for air circulation and
air flow, Oloid-Tech AG
Basel, 2022

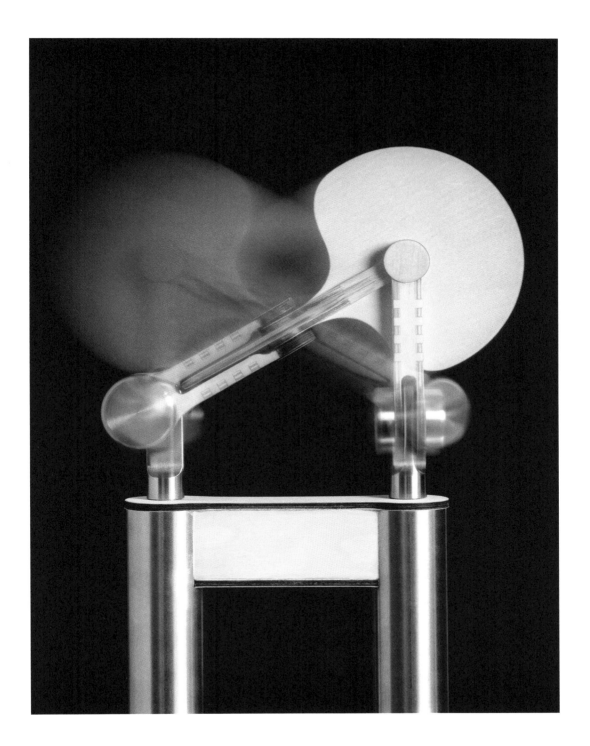

17   Unleashing the dance of life

center of anthroposophy. Schatz was member of this society along with many industrialists of that time, for example the Siemens manager Peter von Siemens, a friend of the Schatz family.

Paul Schatz put an oloid in the water for the first time one day in January 1937. On the reservoir above the Augster Rhine hydroelectric power plant near Basel, he drove a small boat using a hand crank on a prototype made of sheet copper. Due to his enthusiasm, he cranked so vehemently that the boat stared oscillating and ended up capsizing. The inventor almost died after this successful test since he fell into the icy water. Thirty-one years later, he successfully registered a patent for the oloid shape and its technical use in Switzerland. The document dated August 3, 1968, bears the symbolic number 500,000.

left
Paul Schatz demonstrating the division of the cube into cube belt and star bodies, 1960s

right
A rather whimsical application of the invertible cube for advertising purposes by a retailer – three pairs of ladies' shoes carry out an inversion movement in the display window of a shoe store, 1933

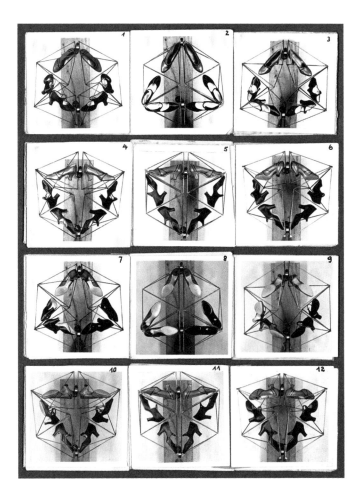

Unleashing the dance of life

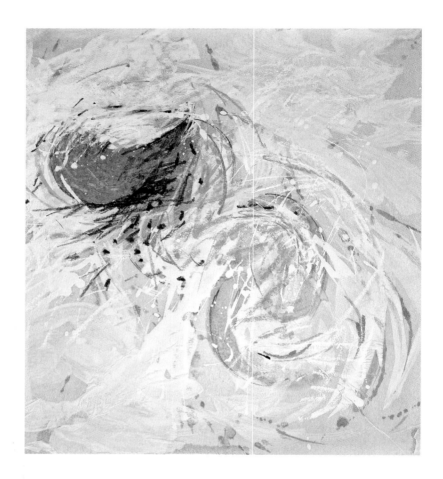

The inverted cube is a symbol as well as a method. Schatz identified the vehicle he needed for his vision of universal renewal. He had plans to use it to power ships, whip cream, clean the air, break down radioactivity, fly, or revitalize the Rhine. At a time when the word environmental pollution was not even been born yet, he had water from the Rhine brought to his studio and used it for experiments in an aquarium. He realized that even the smallest rotating oloids could swirl large quantities of water, increasing the oxygen supply and stimulating microorganisms.

Understanding the oloid requires a truly universal mind, just like its invention. The Swiss artist and singer Linard Bardill calls it a rebirth, a metamorphosis, the process of being alive in life: "The oloid is the visible part of this, an enchanting shape rather than a frightening one."

Oloid study by Marion
Ehrsam, 2019

Oloid

The inversion, he says, brings the cube into a new, formerly unimagined shape. Edges move and form curves, resulting in an object, wonderful looking and novel in its features. Bardill was one of the co-founders of the World Ethic Forum in Pontresina, Switzerland, in summer 2022, where people from all over the world came together to discuss a fundamental change that would have a long-term impact on economy, politics, and society. The oloid and inversion served as key ideas and approaches to initiate the renewal.

Change through fresh thinking

Inversion as answer for a future worth living in – if it unleashes the dance of life, as Bardill puts it: "Paul Schatz has revealed a secret of matter, technology, and man by means of inversion, he created an irritation that allows new synapses to emerge and connect." This is how fresh thinking is produced, this is how change occurs.

The theoretical or experimental ideas of Paul Schatz are today present in many ways: Tobias Langscheid, grandson of Paul Schatz, established the Inversions-Technik GmbH that produces oloid systems at the Alfred Rexrodt company of Berlin, which are used to treat ponds in Australia, wastewater at the Comeco meat company in Belgium, the marine aquarium in Wilhelmshaven, Germany, slurry ponds on

Artist and singer Linard Bardill with the invertible cube, Basel 2022

Hungarian cattle farms, and rainwater catchment basins in Pinneberg, Germany. Currently, more than 1,000 oloids are in use in water treatment around the world.

Kuboid GmbH, founded by Tobias and his brother Christoph Langscheid, sells lamps in the beautiful design of an oloid, all kinds of invertible geometric shapes and other products from Paul Schatz's legacy. The Swiss company 3D Wind AG launched the first 3D wind turbine 'VAYU', whose blades reproduce the movement of oloids. Likewise, sales of the 'Rhythmixx' – an oloid laboratory and kitchen mixer with crank drive – have started. The ‚Water Impulse' project, again set up by Tobias Langscheid with the support of the Paul Schatz Foundation, carries on another of his grandfather's most important projects: the idea of using oloids to move boats while protecting shorelines and canal boundaries and improving water quality at the same time. The maintenance of inland waterways is very expensive because the waves caused by big ship propellers of barges affect the shore structures. For instance, in Venice, the waves produced by the many boat engines drag down the historic fabric of the buildings. If the vaporetti were oloid-driven, the historic buildings could be protected – and so could the water quality.

Or the Heliodome by Éric Wasser – the Alsatian claims he lives in an oloid. His house is located in the small village of Cosswiller in

Éric Wasser in front of his Heliodome passive solar house in Cosswiller, France, 2021

Alsace, near Strasbourg. The architecture emulates the daily and yearly cycle of the sun. This is rather complicated to explain – If the sky was photographed at the same time of day and from the same place during one entire year, the sun would depict a figure eight if all the photos were superimposed. If you cut this picture into slices and build a house out of it, it looks like Éric Wasser's house. It resembles a flying saucer that has landed on edge. The large window front on one side captures the sun's course of the day from the first to the last minute, the space inside is large. And indeed, if the artist Christo would wrap the house, you would see the shape of an oloid.

A new kind of sensitivity

Paul Schatz usually developed his ideas in a coffee house, where he always sat at the same table. His fantastic projects and inexhaustible inventions brought the family to the brink of economic collapse. Schatz had practically no income, neither pension nor health insurance. "Sold the Brockhaus today," his diary reported. It's a watch another time. Next, many years of work get lost because he could no longer afford the rent for a warehouse.

Science, spirituality, art – for Paul Schatz, it all belonged together.

All this is part of a kind of sensibility that is the opposite of the rational, scientific cult of measurability. While this sounds nice, it requires explanation, also in terms of technical parameters. However, the flow behavior of rotating oloids is not yet fully known. Therefore, it is necessary to experience, try out and live what can hardly be explained with words and formulas.

Prof. Martin Wagner of Darmstadt University of Technology and Honorary Professor of Tonqji University Shanghai is a recognized expert in wastewater treatment, ventilation and gas transfer. One of the first scientists to experiment with oloids, he tested oloids in a glass tank with a capacity of 17 cubic meters to determine their level of mixing intensity and the energy required to achieve it. The small aggregates actually moved astonishing amounts of water using just a fraction of the energy of conventional agitators. Mixing liquids this way is essential for sewage treatment plants, for example. Wagner sees another positive aspect in this gentle method of turbulence: In water treatment, precipitants are used that cause fine flakes. These are destroyed by excessively powerful agitators and impair the treatment process, which is why Wagner considers oloids to be ideally suited for wastewater treatment.

Developing countries could particularly benefit from the oloid. The solar-powered oloid unit is already available for a few thousand euros, it could be run at very low operating costs and almost self-sufficiently

Unleashing the dance of life

Oloid

Paul Schatz at his
studio, 1968

Unleashing the dance of life

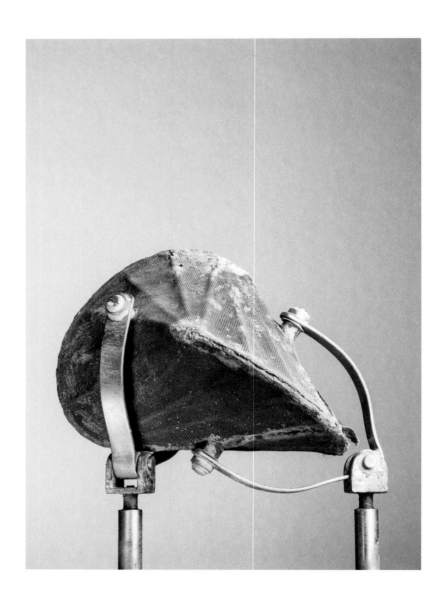

Oloid with fine strainer shell and colloidal silver for the efficient sterilization and purification of water, 1973

in sewage treatment plants or polluted water. However, oloids are now also used in complex industries, such as the paper and chemical industries. Similarly, they are employed in large seawater aquariums, such as the one in Wilhelmshaven, where an oloid gently swirls the water of the shark tank.

Oloid

Vitality in being alive

These examples show that the oloid is now more than a mere concept or vision: inversion is becoming a real and usable option. Yet the oloid, and thus Paul Schatz's philosophy, is not another world-saving model to be repeated. Linard Bardill instead compares it to the image of the fire keeper who sets out to enter into a conversation with the world in the best sense, to make a change of perspective: "I call it the principle of sharing vitality. We don't just look at ourselves as human beings, but we consider all life as equal. For not only we, but everything around us is alive too. So how do we read economics, culture, art and science in the context of this approach?"

The oloid and the concept of inversion are the right platform to initiate universal exchange, with the capital market, the economy, society, science, architecture and art, and all institutions. It is time to use this platform to propel the renewal of the world.

Edge cuboid and oloid as shell volumes, Paul Schatz, um 1967

Unleashing the dance of life

About the
crystals
"building and
habitation"

Paul Schatz

Bauen ┼ Wohnen

4

Not only the relationship between construction and habitation of human beings, but also equivalent relationships in nature, e.g. between bird and nest, between bee and honeycomb, are subject to a primordial phenomenon, which is the essence of any kind of housing creation. In human architecture it is the desire for style, in the animal kingdom it is the reliable instinct of creatures, and in crystal forms it is the law of harmony.

This law focuses on the housing function expanded into an inward and outward reaching progression. It calls attention to the fact that, comparatively speaking, the tree "houses" the nest, the forest the tree, the bird the egg, and the egg the brood. The nest is the dividing line. The way inside progresses via creatures into the organic, while the way outside extends via nature into the cosmic, and there is harmony between the bird and the tree, between the egg and the world. It is precisely this kind of correlation, the type that can be proven with mathematical exactness, which formally relates crystals to each other. It is the relationship between form as content and form as enclosure of that structure which is to crystals what the house is to humans, the nest to birds, the honeycomb to bees. The structure for crystal forms is the cube.

To illustrate this law by a characteristic example, the author created in his "Dornach studio for transparent teaching tools for space and crystal geometry", among other things, the structure which he named "stellar cube" and that was illustrated on the title page of the third number of this journal.

The stellar cube disrupts the one-sided casing conception of the cube by developing it from the alternating interpenetration of two axially symmetrical pyramids. These three-sided pyramids constitute the solid corners of the cube. The 6 tetrahedral "ears" surrounding it extend the cube to a star. It is possible to create countless solids this way, which differ from the stellar cube only by the fact that the interpenetrating physical corners are steeper or flatter than those of the cube. The result is either a steep or a flat rhombohedron.

The two most radical forms of this transformation, which the author calls "rhombohedral transmutation", are on the one hand a linear construct with a prismatic structure, on the other hand a flat structure with hexagonal or hexagramniate limit. They represent the most extreme varieties of crystal forms, which are either needle-shaped or tabular. It is worth mentioning that two types of rhombohedra transmutations, one steeper and one flatter in relation to the stellar cube, belong together, firstly because the trigonometric functions of the angles determining the shapes yield an always constant product, and secondly because the ratios of the factors taken into account

First published in:
'Bauen + Wohnen', Vol.
1–5 (1947–1949), H. 6,
pp. 54–55

left
Star cube on the cover of
'Bauen+Wohnen', issue
3/1948, designed by Paul
Richard Lohse

About the crystals "building and habitation"

are rational. This pairwise affiliation of a steeper and a flatter variety of the rhombohedral transmutation refers to shapes that occur as crystal forms in nature on the one hand, and to proportions that underlie musical intervals on the other.

The ratios applicable to the cube components themselves (ratios which are to be taken as factors on the one hand) have the value √2:2, thus as such they do not correspond to any tonal relation, but rather to the most atonal interval – the so-called tritone (approximately c-f sharp). But the ratio of two such equal ratios, and this equality is characteristic for the cube, provides the proportion 1:1 corresponding to the prime.

Similar to the equality of the characteristic factors of the cube, the angle of inclination between two faces of the cube is equal to the angle between two edges of the cube, both being 90°. This equality exists only in the case of the cube. In all other variations of the rhombohedra transmutation, the angles of inclination of the faces are different from the angles enclosed by two edges of the pyramid. But the product of these two angle values (more exactly: the product 54 of the corresponding trigonometric functions always gives the same value 1:2).

Only once this 1:2 ratio appears both as a result and as a quotient of the characteristic values of the rhombohedron pairs, namely as a manifestation of the fact that the two most extreme varieties mentioned above, the needle-shaped and the table-shaped ones, belong together. Therefore, as the cube in its three-dimensional totality represents the prime ratio, so this togetherness represents the octave ratio.

A closer look reveals that the steeper shapes have their spatial geometric location inside the cube, the flatter shapes outside the cube. If we penetrate two angles of the body with such a degree of steepness that the resulting star rhombohedron is enclosed by the cube with the cube becoming the enveloping body of the resulting star rhombohedron, we get to that tetrahedron penetration known as Kepler's stella octangula, which represents one of the most important structural models in crystallography, e.g. that of pure carbon, the diamond.

If we take two flat angles of the body to penetrate in such a way that the resulting rhombohedron just becomes the enveloping body of the stellar cube, we arrive at that angle of the body which, for example, appears in the garnet crystal (in the garnet ether) as its (so-called three-cornered) angle that also corresponds to the form used by bees to close off their honeycombs inside the hive.

The characteristic values of these two forms have the ratio of the fifth 2:5.

Even though within the scope of these observations the considered law can only be hinted at, its quintessence may nevertheless become clear enough, namely that where nature applies its principles most strictly, i.e. in the mineral kingdom, it strives with absolute necessity for a harmonic conformity between the content and the envelope of its forms.

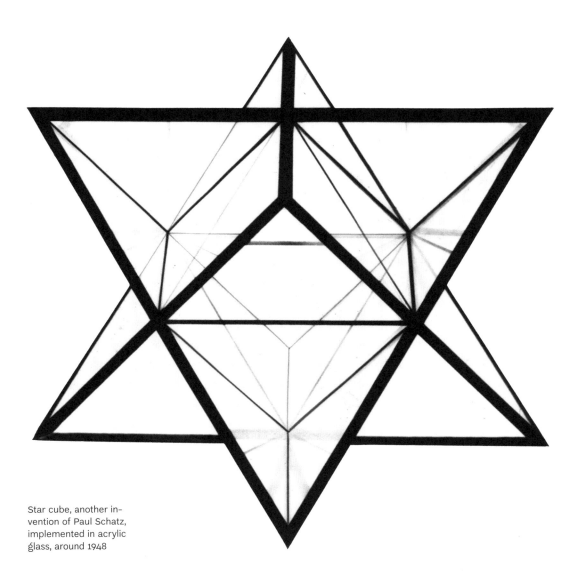

Star cube, another invention of Paul Schatz, implemented in acrylic glass, around 1948

About the crystals "building and habitation"

The poly-somatic sculpture

On the foundation of new stereometric figures

Paul Schatz

5

Paul Schatz calls his series of solids cast in plaster and numerous others, which still are to be discovered in a geometry that has never been exercised, "Umstülpungskörper" (inverted solids): because it is the volumes that are affected by the inversion movement (see werk magazine 12/1962). Their shape retains some of the dynamics of their creation; as a circumscribing space, however, they rest in themselves and could be considered, for example, architectural or hollow forms. The following pages were also published on the occasion of Paul Schatz's 70th birthday, which he celebrated in Dornach on December 22, 1968. Ed.

In its December 1962 issue, the subscribers of werk magazine received an introduction to the "Invertible Cube" (Umstülpbarer Würfel) and its author through an article written by Lucius Burckhardt: "Gestaltungen abseits vom Strom" ("Designs apart from mainstream").

The invertible cube is the most representative extraordinary example of inversions of an infinite number of rhythmically pulsating polyhedra.

The same way polygons made of linear elements are situated in the plane and polyhedra made of plane figures in space, polysomes (as the author calls such invertible systems) made of solids are located in time.

We are aware that a polygon in a plane constitutes a planimetric wholeness and that a polyhedron figure does the same in space. It is, however, not easy to grasp the polysome in its entirety. To move from the polyhedron (in space) to the polysome (in time) we have to comprehend the movement of the invertible polyhedron returning to its starting point, as a superordinate whole. The polysomatic sculpture is perception of the form enhanced to the level of visual integration, projected into three-dimensional space by the polysome.

The polysome sculpture can serve first to implant the consciousness with a perceptive ability towards temporal forms. In addition, it is part of spatial geometry in general, because it constitutes new stereometric figures. The way they come into being obeys mathematical laws. They differ fundamentally from well-known stereometric figures by the way they develop. Hence, they play a remarkably unique role in the realm of solids. This exceptional role is based on the ability to perceive shapes produced by time, which emerges when the sense of space is combined with knowledge of the theorem.

The most representative figures of stereometry are the sphere, the cone and the cube (the ellipsoid is a variety of the sphere, the cylinder of the cone, and the cuboid of the cube). What in stereometry is the sphere or hemisphere appears in architecture as a dome, the

*First published in:
Das Werk: Architektur
und Kunst. Vol. 56 (1969),
H. 1 'Einfamilienhäuser,
Ferienhäuser', p. 4–7*

left
Natural stone oloid of
the Breton sculptor
Christophe Chini, 2023

The polysomatic sculpture

cylinder as a round tower, the cube or cuboid as the basic form of the megaron of architecture, which has dominated architecture since ancient Greek times.

There is a painting by Niklaus Stoecklin from 1927 (in the Kunstmuseum Winterthur, Switzerland), which shows these three solids: sphere, cone, and cube, in their magnificent dignity like three abstract gods. It is gratifying to see that they find artistic recognition (outside of the pedantic representation of geometry) at a time when they no longer rule the realm of space studies.

Thanks to their mathematical transparency, the figures of stereometry are of fundamental importance in architecture. In terms of structural analysis, they underpin the tectonics of design from a rational point of view. Obviously, we can only speak of architecture if the formal expression is in line with the spirit of the building.

New stereometric figures emerging from the polysome are located on the same borderline with architecture because they obey strict mathematical laws as well.The generators of the enveloping surfaces under consideration can be calculated as straight lines through static analysis. However, they have a far more three-dimensional character than the traditional shapes of stereometry. Only the hyperbolic paraboloid (the saddle surface) has a distant relationship to the polysomatic forms. Since they appeal to the sense for spatial art by their amazing beauty, it is tempting to speak of variants of the art of Mathesis, as Haeckel did of variants of the art of nature, even though both are contradictions in terms.

There is only one cube, but an uncountable number of cuboids. Similarly, there are also an infinite number of polysomatic forms and we are presenting the most fundamental ones that originate from

The half pole cuboid

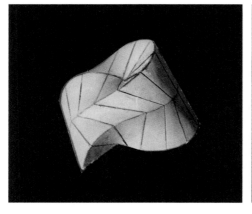
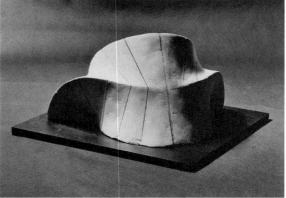

Oloid

the invertible cube. This term is based on the following: The form results from five interplaying central cube edges with one central edge held in position. Fig. 2 [fig. p.34] shows only the half edge cuboid. This is related to the entire object like the dome to the sphere. Placed on a reflecting surface, the whole body becomes visible. The lines in the figure are the central axes of the invertible cube belt in sequential 13 positions of the inversion. The same applies to the half pole cuboid with a cup-shaped ground plan. One pole edge is fixed and the connecting central edges move symmetrically to the diagonal of the cube. Probably,

The polysomatic sculpture

there will be better terms to describe the most elementary polysomatic solids. The half pole cuboid with a cup-shaped ground plan could be called an inversion hall, for example.

The half pole cuboid with circular ground plan

This design is identical to the previous one in terms of spatial geometry, what becomes clear at once when placing both the inverted hall and the inverted dome (that's how the half pole cuboid with circular ground plan could be called) on a reflecting surface. The polysomatic sculpture in this example was created without linear generators. Only this process leads to the experience of the three-dimensional shape created by time, because this shape is not created by a finite but by an infinite number of positions of the inversion movement states.

The Oloid

The oloid is a structure which differs from the previous ones by one essential property. Its generators are not 5 or 6 cube edges, but a single diagonal of the cube. The middle central edge of the half chain of central edges of the invertible cube belt consisting of three middle edges is fixed. In terms of spatial geometry, this structure belongs to

The oloid, 1969

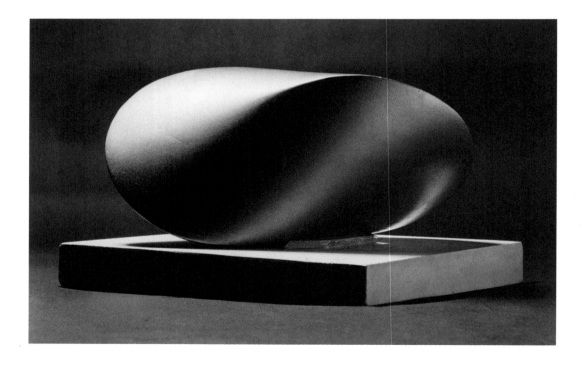

Oloid

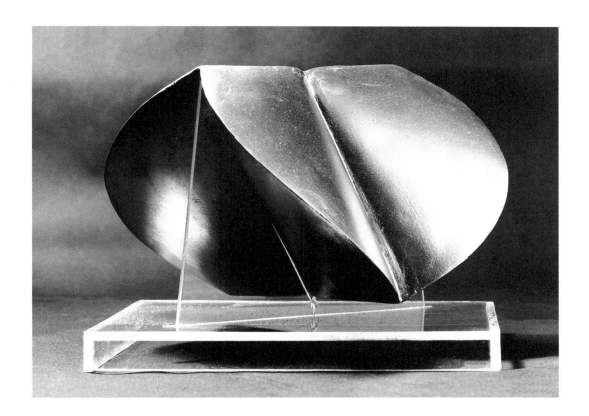

the genus of connecting torses of two circles that can be unrolled. Its development method described here is practically unknown and has so far not been recognized by spatial geometry.

It is a rolling element that rolls rhythmically pulsating on the flat ground, i.e. with four times changing distances to it.

The four-chamber body of the cube inversion

This four-chamber body arises from the motion interplay of two sections of the cube diagonals of the middle edge chain of the cube, when fixing the edge of the cube from whose end the diagonals start. The method of creation of the bodies depicted by means of five examples here is an entry into the field of polysomatic sculpture from the most elementary point of view of kinematics of inversion. We are dealing with kinetic forms which, on the one hand, are subject to a strict order, but which, nevertheless, combined with creative imagination, take us to the unlimited realm of plastic design.

The four-chambered body of the cube inversion, 1969

The polysomatic sculpture

38   Oloid

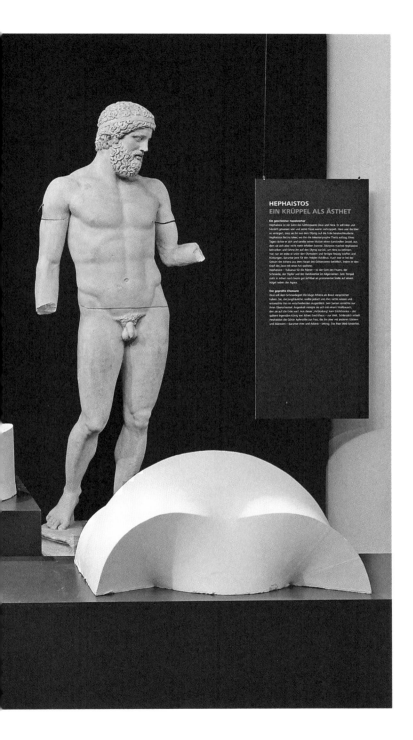

Polysomatic bodies
according to Paul Schatz
in front of plaster casts
of antique sculptures of
Zeus, Hera and Hepha-
estus, exhibition at Skulp-
turenhalle Basel during
the Architekturwoche
Basel 2023

The polysomatic sculpture

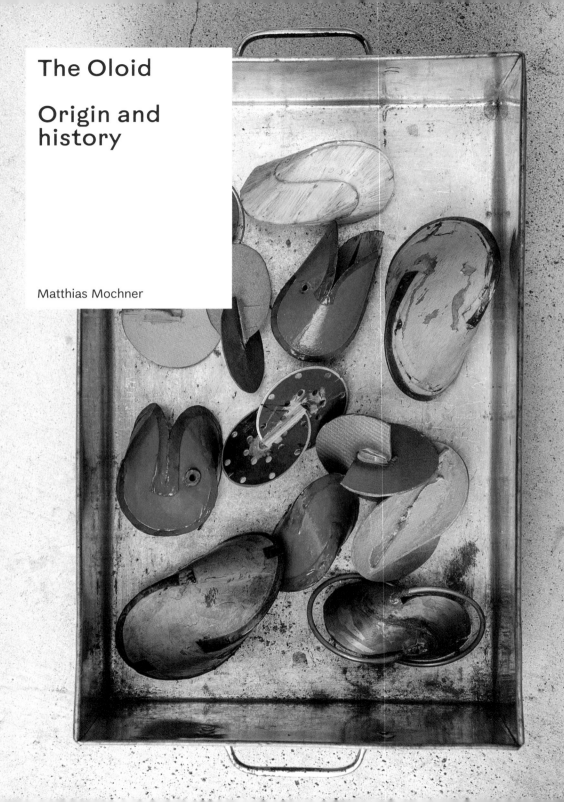

The Oloid

Origin and history

Matthias Mochner

6

«Wenn der Bildner die Gebilde
Freundlich zur Erscheinung ruft
Mußt du wohl in stille[r] Milde
Überprüfen was du schufst.»¹

(When the creator in a friendly manner asks the created forms to appear, you must quietly and gently test what you have created.)

The oloid is not a "solid" body, it is movement, i.e. it "arises" as a shape developing over time from the central belt section of a cube. This shape developing over time can be formed as a solid body – and can be used in technology. Nevertheless, it originates in the realm of things developing over time. When did Paul Schatz mention the oloid for the first time?

In June/July 1931, he wrote an essay entitled *Betrachtungen allgemeiner Art* (General observations) where he mentions and outlines an "almond-shaped polysomatoloid."² This was a good year and a half after discovery of the inversion. A pencil sketch made before March 26, 1930 shows the two circular disks standing crosswise to each other, which are assumed to be known to the readers of his essay, lovingly described (as inversion rudders) and sketched³ in relation to earth,

left
A box containing oloids made by Paul Schatz, now kept in his estate

right
Pencil sketch of two circular disks standing in a cross position to each other, before March 26, 1930

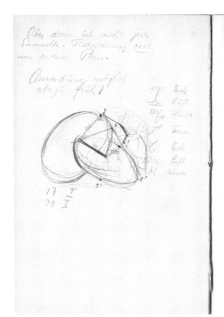

The Oloid

water air and fire. He commented his sketch: "Application possible, but too early?"[4] Since Schatz wrote on June 19, 1930, that he had "succeeded in storing the serpoloid",[5] and thus was familiar with the term "oloid" as a word fragment, therefore it may be assumed that the term "oloid" was born before March 1930. Schatz's statement of January 12, 1931, next to the sketch of a cube and the oloid, is revealing: "The cross circle wheel / The serpentine wheel / I was already looking for that a year ago."[6] The concept was thus established since late January 1930.

A pencil sketch of an oloid moving in the air, called "The Air Shoe," is dated January 21, 1931.[7] On January 7, 1931, Schatz writes about a "bicolloloid",[8] although the creation of this word itself was a problem for him, since he separated the word elements using vertical strokes. A wonderful, tiny pencil sketch from early January 1931 shows an upright floating oloid expressing, as it were, its very essence. On the right side he wrote "Easy mobility!"[9] And, as if he wanted to grasp this realization more accurately, he drew two beings (human beings?) facing each other – and between them an oloid. Below he wrote: "Horizontal to itself / Vertical from the other" (left) and "Vertical to itself / Horizontal from the other" (right). This was his attempt was to characterize the polar qualities of movement in their interplay, i.e. "The movement of the surface."[10]

left
"Easy mobility!", upright floating oloid, May 30, 1931

right
Drawing of the oloid, around January 2, 1931

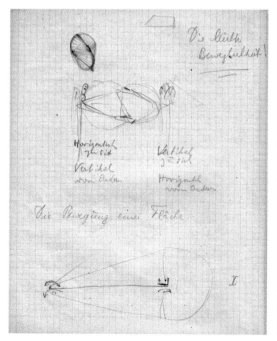

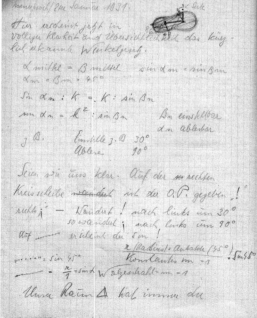

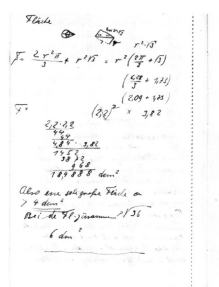

Two oloids, used as ship propulsion, September 19, 1932

Research in January 1931 also calls the oloid "the tumbling wheel." "The work has made good progress. The tumbling wheel will be considered as a drilling and digging wheel / as an air pump and as a tumbling wing structure. It could be designed as a model of an airplane!."[11] Schatz struggled particularly with the mathematical calculation and penetration of the movement process, as documented in various sketches that were accompanied by calculations.[12] Around January 2, 1931, these efforts culminated in an oloid sketch next to the sentence: "Here now the recently discovered angle rule appears very clearly and easy to see."[13]

At the turn of the year 1930/1931 he noted: "I am happy about the progress of the centrally connected hexasomatic half-cylinder. Something new is about to enter the process of clarifying consciousness."[14] Moreover: "This structure is making a motion of weirdly combined movements. Partly a plane is gliding as a plane / The radial rays are turning. The axis is rotating – I still cannot imagine it. I have to create and *know* the created only after its creation. Isn't this a proof that I am entering the field of forces? Or perhaps my imaginative capacity is weak."[15] On February 16, 1931, Schatz stated that the "idea of my hemihexosomatoloid (...) as such" must stop because it is "too expensive."[16] Once again, the oloid is a word fragment here. A pencil sketch from May 30, 1931 shows the wheel cross, with the two wheels being slightly pulled apart.[17]

A pencil sketch from September 19, 1932, already depicts two oloids used as ship propulsion (not as inverted rotors as in 1931). In a biographical review of the year 1935 Schatz noted for the year 1930: "Probably progressive achievements in the field of inversion mechanics. Late 30 Polysomatoloids."[18]

After 1933 Schatz continued to "move" the oloid, initially in an attempt to use it for ship propulsion. Research of this dated between 1933 and 1938, had to be abandoned because no suitable research laboratories were available in Switzerland and the journey to Germany was impossible due to his Jewish background, which meant that the "ship was left high and dry", as he put it in retrospect in the essay "The Oloid as an Organ of Repulsion" 35 years later.[19] Schatz was looking for mechanisms of movement suitable to use in water: "At the time, one of the things I was looking at was how trout move about.[20] Studies of this kind prompted me to build a small model, which I repeatedly exhibited to interested persons in swimming pools or, if necessary, in bathtubs as early as 1933."[21] Those "interested persons" included the most renowned researchers in Switzerland.[22] In 1938, test drives took place on the Augster reservoir with "a test boat (...) manufactured by me."[23] On February 26, 1941, the oloid is mentioned in Schatz's pocket diary, e.g. in sketches for flying objects.[24]

The same year, the patent application for a "water vehicle" propelled by means of oloids is submitted.[25] In the 1940s, inflatable

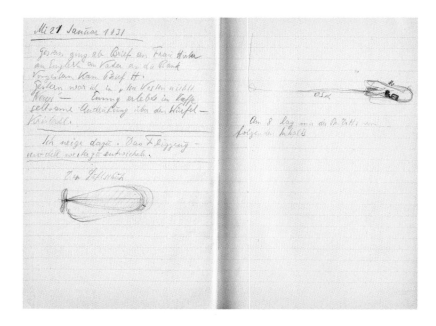

Flying object sketches,
February 26, 1941

Oloid

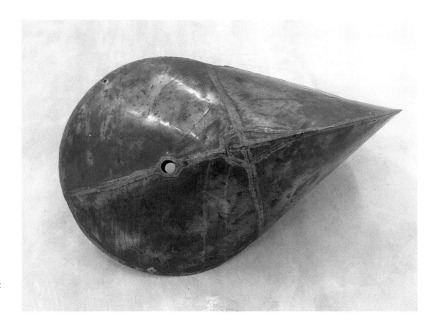

An 80 centimeter-long oloid used by Paul Schatz as a ship's propulsion system in 1937

oloids were created, and as early as 1936, there are graphic attempts to develop a signet from the oloid, which once again documents the importance Schatz attributed to this solid.[26] Delicate drawings in color illustrating the development of the oloid date from September 1951.[27]

After the great success of the "Turbula" mixer in the early 1960s, Schatz once again turned his attention to the study and further development of the oloid. Much of what became possible seemed to be the result of work that had been carried on in silence for decades, now coming to light transformed in a kind of mirror image of the work of the early 1930s.

Between the years 1967 and 1969, decisive achievements were made: a sieve oloid was developed, and the introduction of ozone into water by using oloids was investigated. On August 3, 1968, an application for a patent for technical applications of the oloid was submitted. Through a chain of lucky events, the Swiss patent was assigned the number 500,000. In 1973, the German public broadcaster WDR produced a television documentary about Schatz's life and work. As a result, the inverted cube (or more precisely, an inverting chain of cubes) became WDR's broadcasting logo. In the early 1970s, Schatz began work at the laboratory of the ETH Zurich.[28] There he started to focus on water sanitation by means of oloids. In this area, as he wrote in 1976: "The main reason for my research was and is to create

The Oloid

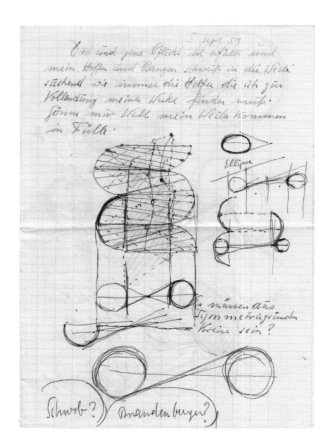

mechanisms that do not have any harmful effects on nature."[29] The oloid received increasing attention, became better known and popular as a solid figure – at the same time, new work sprouted in modesty and silence. Little is known about it yet, so far barely known devices are testimonies of the research of that time. A good year before his death, Schatz shared his thoughts in a draft letter of February 15, 1978 with Silvius Dornier (b. 1927): "Recently, I came across the solution that allows me to carry out the long overdue determination of the oloid's maritime efficiency."[30]

The term oloid was formulated by Schatz in a complex and multi-layered process a few months after the discovery of inversion. Its form was "felt" in the course of many years, calculated, reflected – its essence emerging from the increasingly in-depth exploration of the inversion of the cube. This path conditioned the presentation of the oloid, of the polysomatic design, but also of the oloidic forma-

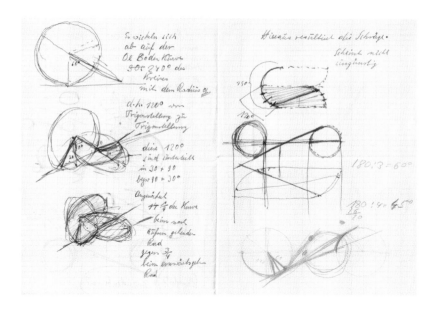

tions in his book *Rhythmusforschung und Technik* (1975). This was a final, difficult attempt to make the oloid and his own life's work accessible to the public in a general overview.[31] An attempt that — to return to the inversion of the cube, the origin of the oloid — is the result of a research method that links heaven and earth. Schatz noted on Sunday, January 29, 1950: "Is it possible to relate the electron distances to the inversion of the cube and to deduct proportions for distances between stars from this? The invertible cube as a model to demonstrate density mass volume temperature?"[32]

1 PSS — 01 01.05. Beginning of a chronicle by Schatz dated June 7, 1932.
2 Mochner, Schatz, 2016, p. 82 with fig. 23.
3 Mochner, Schatz, 2016, p. 82 with fig. 21.
4 PSS — 01.01.04.
5 PSS — 01.01.04.
6 PSS — 01.01.04.
7 PSS — 01.01.04.
8 PSS — 01.01.04.
9 PSS — 01.01.04.
10 PSS — 01.01.04. At this point there are several additional sketches of the oloid shape.
11 PSS — 01.01.04.
12 PSS — 01.01.04.
13 PSS — 01.01.04.
14 PSS — 01.01.04.
15 PSS — 01.01.04.
16 PSS — 01.01.04.
17 PSS — 01.01.04.
18 PSS — 01.01.03.
19 Mochner, Schatz, 2016, p. 437.
20 Corresponding works can be found in Schatz's library.
21 Mochner, Schatz, 2016, p. 437.
22 For example the shipbuilding engineer Adolf J. Ryniker (1875–1960).
23 The first trail run was on January 19, 1938.
24 Mochner, Schatz, 2016, p. 391.
25 Mochner, Schatz, 2016, p. 438–439.
26 Mochner, Schatz, 2016, p. 375.
27 Mochner, Schatz, 2016, p. 347.
28 Mochner, Schatz, 2016, p. 446, fig. 549.
29 Mochner, Schatz, 2016, p. 444.
30 PSS — 01.04.69.
31 Mochner, History, 2013, p. 127–136.
32 PSS — 01.02.02.

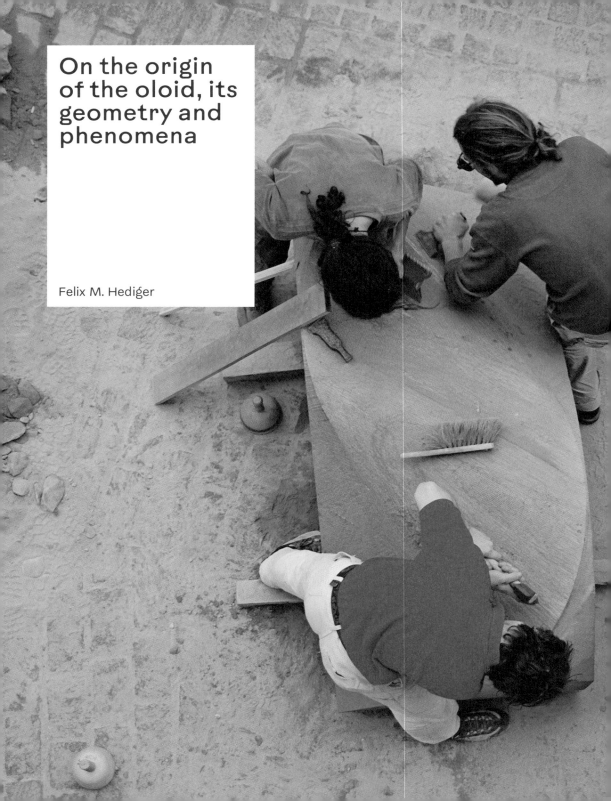

On the origin of the oloid, its geometry and phenomena

Felix M. Hediger

7

The discovery of the oloid by Paul Schatz contains many aspects and properties that I will refer to as phenomena because in this context they are particularly fascinating and move us profoundly in many ways. The discovery of the oloid was a result of Paul Schatz's holistic imaginative attitude and personality. His extensive mathematical-geometrical, astronomical, artistic, as well as spiritual knowledge and affinities equipped him to adequately access the topic. This essay intends to illustrate that it is possible to refer to the oloid as a geometric phenomenon. The discussion could also focus on the magic and grace of this form, its artistic aspect, i.e. the emotional experience of the shape, or on its spiritual component, exploring the universal and fundamental nature of the inversion process. However, while my discussion will hint at some of these holistic aspects, I will limit myself primarily to a geometric consideration.

The geometrical phenomenal side of the oloid genesis

Paul Schatz found a way to divide the cube into eight adjacent segments and thus make it moveable. In doing so, six tetrahedral segments are connected to each other, but remain movable. Each of these elements culminates in three cube edges and is joined to two adjacent segments in a hinge-like manner, resulting in a movable chained ring (Fig. p. 50a.l.). This so-called cube belt is the starting point of the oloid genesis. The two other cube segments, not yet described, are assigned to the two cube edges, and form a pole pair, so to speak, while the cube belt constitutes the equator, so to speak (Fig. p. 50a.r.). Only when these two cube corners are removed, does the cube belt become movable. Interestingly, the corner segments are equal in volume to the complete cube belt. They each share exactly 1/3 of the volume of the cube. Another phenomenon of this geometrical constellation concerns the three cube diagonals connected to the cube belt (Fig. p. 50b.). They don't change their length during the movement of the cube belt! This geometrical-phenomenal property already takes us to the heart of the creation of the oloid, because all three diagonals of the cube belt in motion shape an oloid in their movement. That means, the oloid shape (resp. its hull surface) arises as a geometric locus of the diagonals moving over a stationary cube belt segment. Thus, we fixate one of the tetrahedral segments and move the rest of the segments around it while observing the movement of the diagonal that is not connected to the fixed element.

The oloid results from this path, i.e. the diagonal "cuts" the oloid shape out of the space. Thus, the oloid's outer hull is the geometrical locus of this moving diagonal (Fig. p. 51). For those who cannot visualize these complex geometrical relations or who want to check

Production of a sandstone oloid during the event week in front of the Unternehmen Mitte in Basel on the occasion of the 80th anniversary of the discovery of the invertible cube, 2009

On the origin of the oloid, its geometry and phenomena

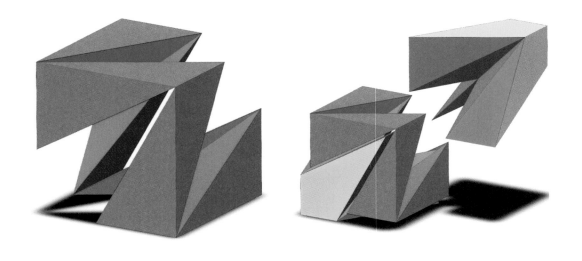

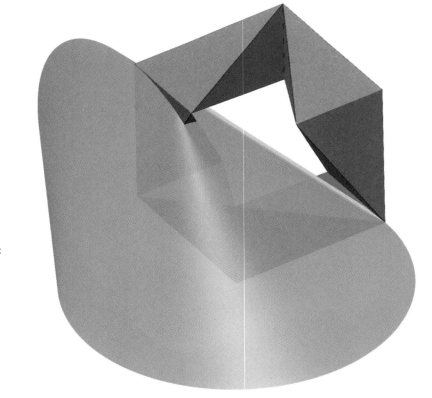

above left
Cube belt consisting of six
cube sections connected
like hinges

above right
The cube belt and the
two star bodies with the
extra cube edges

below
Cube belt displaying a
diagonal line (green line)

Oloid

their visualization, I have posted an animated illustration online.[1] It is important to mention, of course, that this diagonal movement, which forms the oloid, is related to a very specific movement of the cube belt. Paul Schatz called this mandatory motion of the cube belt the inverted or inversion motion. The cube belt is able to turn inside out and vice versa. This property can be observed in the stages that the cube belt makes during its movement. In essence, besides its initial and final stages, it goes through three stages during an inversion (Fig. p. 52a.). They all correspond to an exact geometric feature of the cube, acting from the outside. The volume of the cube belt, meanwhile, is located in the space surrounding the cube structure and acts on it almost as if an imaginary cube was created by sculpting it (indicated by lines in the pictures).

Other stages of the cube's inversion, not shown here, also provide clues to rhythmic processes, which are part of the rhythm research coined by Paul Schatz. The oloid also reveals rhythmic qualities, for

Oloid (slightly transparent) with the diagonal (green) of the cube belt running along its surface. Top: the cube belt during its cube phase, bottom: the cube belt moving on

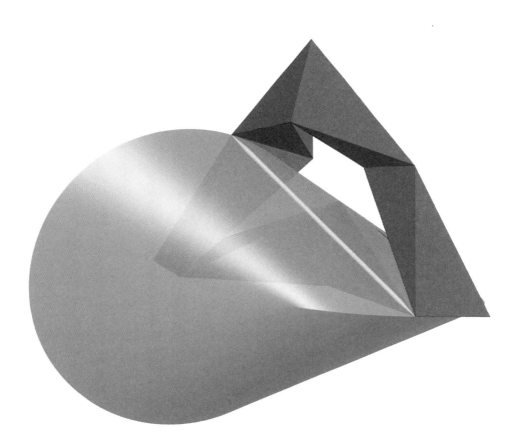

On the origin of the oloid, its geometry and phenomena

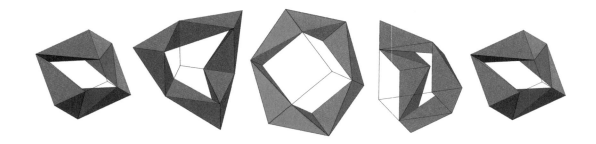

instance with regard to the way it rolls, describing a meandering path with a staggering motion (Fig. p. 52b.).

When it is moved kinematically in exactly the same way as it was created (through so-called inversion kinematics), its rhythmic qualities also become particularly effective and impressive. In other words, the mobility of the cube belt then serves as the motion driver of the oloid. The result is a geometric–organic connection of the oloid form and its derivation, applicable in rhythmic terms. Geometrically, this shows one of the representative forms of movement of rhythm, the lemniscate. It moves the midpoint of the oloid in motion (Fig. p. 53) and this brings us back to the universality of everything that happens around the oloid, because the lemniscate movement is also an expression or the real symbol of inversion. The inversion movement within the spatial reality, intrinsic to the cube belt, follows a toroidal principle of motion, which is universally apparent. Furthermore, many things in life that depend on the rhythmic alternation of the inside and the outside can be assigned to this principle.

Specific qualities and phenomena of the oloid

— The body rolls along its entire surface. There are very few solids besides the oloid that can do this, especially the sphericons.
— The rolling motion follows a compulsive rhythmic sequence (Fig. p. 52b.).
— The oloid is a completely developable form. This means that it can be created from a planar piece solely by bending (Fig. p. 52b.).
— Despite its simple structure, it is not possible to create or derive the process of developing geometrically, but rather only by using mathematics.
— Despite the oloid's complex, somewhat "exploratory," derivation from the cube's inversion, its shape is structurally simple, i.e. it can

above
During a complete inversion from cube to cube (from far left to far right), the transformation from inversion goes through three different stages in which negative cube shapes are formed inside the cube chain.

below
Meandering trajectory and unrolling of the oloid

Oloid

be described only by two circles or segments of circles perpendicular to each other and intersecting each other at both midpoints.

— The oloid's surface is equal to the surface of a sphere whose radius is equal to the radius of the oloid's edges.

— Its inner structure contains the Golden Section (proportion of the continuous division – also called "Divine Proportion") in manifold distinctive form (indicated in Fig. p. 53).

— In the close association with its emergence from the inversion movement, the oloid has the potential to shape an organic-rhythmic technology and it is considered an example of a new organic design method, also founded by Paul Schatz, which he named "polysomatic design."

1 www.vimeo.com/154917442

The lemniscate path (pink) that the oloid midpoint (purple) moves along when it is moved in an inversion kinematic way. The "Golden Section" is a recent discovery on the oloid by the author and an example of various "transcendences" related to the oloid.

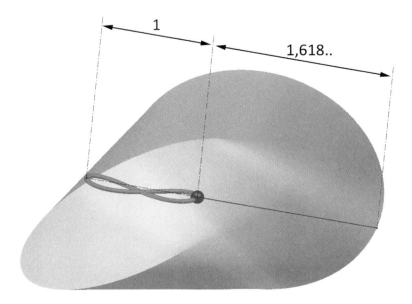

On the origin of the oloid, its geometry and phenomena

Spatial variations: the cuboid oloid

Christoph Müller

8

This chapter deals with the interaction between the oloid and its fundamental geometry: the invertible cube. What kind of shapes emerge when we use a cuboid instead of the cube to develop the oloid?

To examine this inversion, an inverse kinematic solver was used. This method is usually used in robotics to find the fastest way to move robotic arms. It is possible to create virtual joints that can be accordingly constrained in their movement as well.

There are three variations of the inversion: On the left there is a cube with an edge length of 1 × 1 × 1 units. In the middle, its width and height vary, resulting in a cuboid with 1 × 1.2 × 1.2 units. Finally, a cuboid with three varying edge lengths of 1 × 1.2 × 1.4 units is shown on the right.

It could be expected that the variation of the length of the edges culminates in ovals or even free forms. However, on closer inspection, the edges of the oloid rotate around the fixed part of the initial shape, regardless of their edge length. This results in circular segments, similar to the cube belt. Only the radius of these segments and their opening angle change.

The resulting oloids are homogeneous as well. At first glance, only the proportion of the resulting geometry varies.

The juxtaposition of the developed oloids is very exciting. Depending on which edge is modified, the result is a curved instead of a straight development.

Initial position

Spatial variations: the cuboid oloid

Position 2 – Triangle

Position 3 – Cube / Cuboid

Position 4 – Cube / Cuboid

Position 5 – Cube / Cuboid

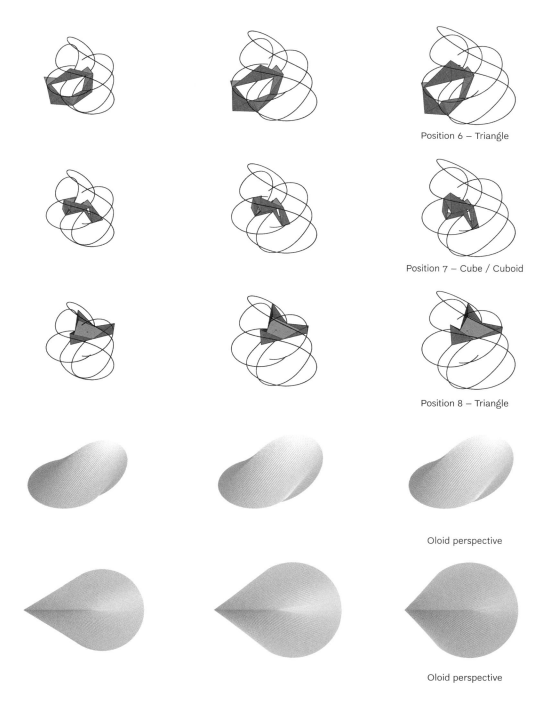

Position 6 – Triangle

Position 7 – Cube / Cuboid

Position 8 – Triangle

Oloid perspective

Oloid perspective

Spatial variations: the cuboid oloid

A special case of inversion occurs when an acute triangle is chosen as starting point. This happens, for example, when there is an edge length of 0.6 × 1.2 × 1.4 units. It can be seen that the center of the triangle is outside the triangle. The result is a cube that is already partially inverted before its inversion. In other words, it is an inversion within the inversion.

In his studies, Paul Schatz examined points that he extended into lines, shaping surfaces and finally creating space. He already developed the oloid further himself by replacing the initial form of the cube by the cuboid, and thus opening up more possibilities. The introductory title image shows the four variations depicted in their spatial connection. They embody the range of possibilities, which is already created by choosing four different versions.

Position 1 – Cuboid

Position 2 – Triangle

Position 3 – Cuboid

Position 4 – Triangle

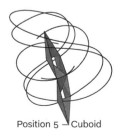
Position 5 – Cuboid

Cube belt and two star bodies according to Paul Schatz

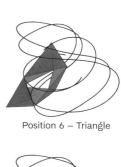

Position 6 — Triangle

Position 7 — Cuboid

Position 8 — Triangle

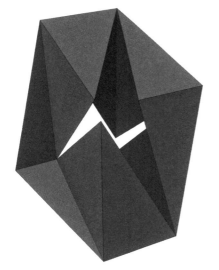

Impossible cuboid

Oloid perspective

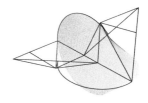

Oloid perspective

Spatial variations: the cuboid oloid

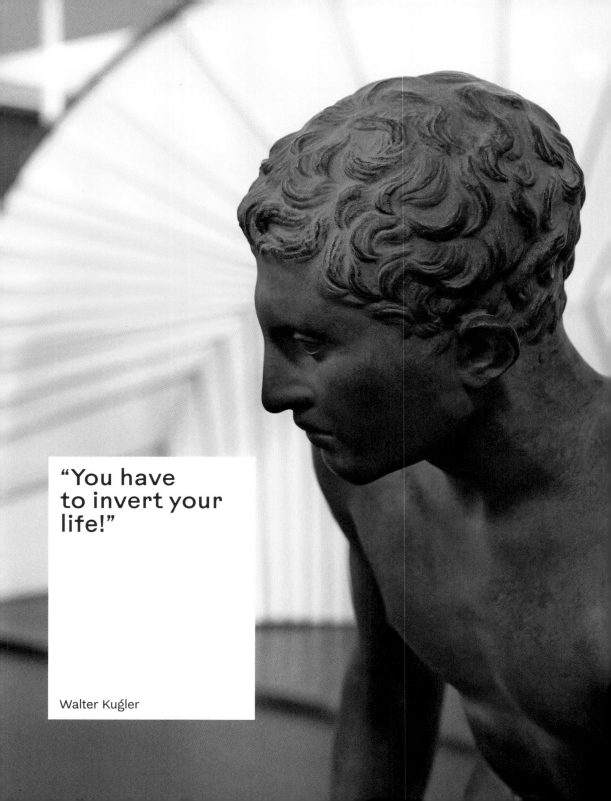

"You have
to invert your
life!"

Walter Kugler

9

In 1920, Robert Musil wrote in his diary "Rationality and mysticism — are the two opposing poles of our times"[1], leaving his imprint in the history of his era. For it was only two years since the young century, so full of promise, had lost its innocence on the battlefields of the First World War. The symbols representing the much talked about belief in progress, transferred so triumphantly from the 19th to the 20th century had suddenly faded; the question of the meaning of life was reduced to mere survival strategies. In his diary entry, the mechanical engineer and writer Musil named the key data of a path leading towards the future and at the same time calls for a broader concept of knowledge and science. Musil's message suggests that any rational world always comes with another world, a non-rational, mystical world, as a partner, and that this should no longer be left to speculation, but should become common knowledge. In this regard, there is still a lot to be worked out today.

Paul Schatz, who was born in Constance, Germany in 1898, was one of the people who fully comprehended this message. First mathematics and the natural sciences drove him, then technology, then art, and finally natural sciences and technology again. Then, somewhere in between, he discovered anthroposophy as a spiritual science that also inherently deals with the scientific and technical aspects of life.

Around 1922 Paul Schatz experienced an inversion of sorts. From then on, things no longer happened successively, but rather simultaneously: natural science, philosophy, anthroposophy, art and technology. He documented his findings and practical experience meticulously in his numerous treatises, on mathematical problems, especially geometry, but also on their technical implementation and, time and again, on art. He was also a hands-on person, as many of his inventions show. For instance, he dedicated himself to the oloid technology used in wastewater treatment as well as water purification, or the turbula mixer, which is "an indispensable tool in laboratories and industrial plants for the processes of deburring, mixing as well as for the production of emulsions."[2]

A key figure during his years of study at the technical universities in Munich and Hanover was Theodor Lessing ("Geschichte als Sinngebung des Sinnlosen", 1919), enfant terrible among the philosophers and lecturers at the university in Hanover, who made a deep impression on Schatz because of his idiosyncratic thinking patterns and raised doubts in him about the common methods of thinking used by the scientific establishment of the time. His search for meaning led him to art, and in 1922 he began an artistic apprenticeship at the woodcarving school in Cieplice Śląskie-Zdrój, Poland. That same year, a lecture by Rudolf Steiner reactivated his interest in natural science. Steiner

Bronze sculpture in front of the inversion pavilion, Skulpturhalle Basel during the Architekturwoche Basel 2022

"You have to invert your life!"

dictated in several variations to his audience that contemporary science uses thinking only as a device and does not grant it any independent creative power: "It has actually become the servant, the mere means for research. Thus thought, as a human experience, is eliminated from the relationship that man has with the world in relation to realities. Thought has become a formal tool to comprehend realities. It is no longer revealing its own self within natural science."[3]

Courage to embrace instability

No matter how much the exact sciences were close to his heart, Paul Schatz first devoted himself to art after his studies. He worked for several years as a sculptor in his own studio near Lake Constance, driven by the desire "to find a way of thinking that is clear, but does not freeze the artistic dimension, and to achieve a true artistic creation that flows from a visible, uncontrollable source – not a dark one."[4] It is, of course, also the postwar period and the early years of the Weimar Republic that make him experience a sometimes

Oloid

unbearable emptiness, what Paul Schatz calls ‚Weltverlorenheit' (world
forlornness), spreading in an unstoppable way: "We have now come
to world forlornness and modern sculpture records this as the mental
reality of our century [...] Modern sculpture proclaims the courage to
embrace instability."[5]

Inspired anew by Steiner, Paul Schatz also began to explore the
connections between modern art and the latest findings in natural
science. Later on, in 1962, he published his observations and reflections
in a series of essays under the main title of *Betrachtungen zur Bildhauerei*. The five-part series of essays begins with a history of material science and an examination of the "aberration of the term element"[6] and
ends with astronomical-cosmological-evolutionary-historical observations, resulting in the statement that in modern times the natural has

"You have to invert your life!"

turned away from the spiritual. He concludes that this turning away will become absurd in the nearest future and "a turning away from that turning away" will take place. To him, the solution to all these problems is derived from the way surfaces of three-dimensional forms are created, i.e. the expression of form in space, and this primordial phenomenon has a language of its own, and this language has an alphabet, and this "alphabet has only two basic letters: Inside and Outside!"

Every time a surface is bent, according to Paul Schatz, "a certain ratio between the inside and the outside emerges, and the inversion of these ratios, making the inside the outside, the outside the inside, are three-dimensional twice bends."[7] In this context, we are dealing with a dynamic process of alternation, with transformation and metamorphosis. Transformation proceeds in time and space, has to do with what is up and what is down, what is visible and not visible, what is inside and what is outside. Transformation is articulated not only

Paul Schatz inverting a
cube belt, 1960s

Oloid

in continuity, but also in discontinuity, takes place through turning in and turning out. In short, the hallmark of transformation is inversion. What is inside one moment is outside the next. Decisive here for every scientist, every artist and every human being in their everyday life is the way of perception and thinking. Finally, Paul Schatz experiences during his mathematical studies that it is important to find the transition from purely mathematical knowledge of form to feeling form, because, according to Steiner: "Feeling the circle in the plane, feeling the sphere in the space, is feeling selfness, is feeling the self."[8] These and other considerations eventually brought Schatz to a type of motion that extended the "basic types of motion of the technical theory of gears: rotation and translation through the rhythmically pulsating inversion." This was preceded by his discovery of the inversion of geometric bodies, especially the cube. This was in 1929 and was also the beginning of the exciting history of inversion technology.

You have to invert your life!

"You must change your life" – this is what the poet Rilke once heard a Greek sculpture utter and in 1907 included in his poem *Archaic Torso of Apollo*. Since then, generations of readers have tried to interpret this invitation and some have probably tried to live it. Yet as liberating as this invitation might be for each and every one of us, it can become just as agonizing if we decide to actually follow it. Change my life? Gladly, but how? Markus Brüderlin had the key: "You have to invert your life!" Brüderlin, longtime curator of the Fondation Beyeler and later director of the Kunstmuseum in Wolfsburg, entered and created exciting terrain in 2010 with the exhibition *Rudolf Steiner and Contemporary Art* together with the artists invited to participate, such as Ólafur Elíasson, Anish Kapoor, Katharina Grosse and others. At the same time, he showed the exhibition *Rudolf Steiner – The Alchemy of Everyday Life*, conceived by the Vitra Design Museum, which "naturally" also features works by Paul Schatz. If you ask Brüderlin why he decided to show both exhibitions at the same time, he, who for decades had been navigating all levels of 20th and 21st century art with his trademark certainty, quickly turned to Rudolf Steiner, because his experience taught him: there is simply no way of avoiding Steiner when it comes to substance. He used to explore the field of tension between the sacred and the profane with apparent effortlessness. It was not about a definition of positions that was susceptible to corrosion, but about interrelationships between mind and matter, inside and outside, and even about inversions. This is what he said in his contribution to the exhibition catalog of the Vitra Design Museum: "In his attempt to depict the relationship between the outer, physical world

"You have to invert your life!"

and the inner, spiritual world, Steiner developed a method of thinking
and feeling that in a peculiar way reflects a fundamental principle of
modern culture, of thinking right through to the practice of design, and
identifies him as a key figure in the dawn of modernity. It is the principle of *inversion*."[9]

By the way: During the 1970s, millions were able to watch the
process of inversion every day on WDR Cologne's television station,

Oloid

right
Mural by Rudolf Steiner, 1923

below
WDR used this station logo in the mid-1970s in the form of an animated inversion movement after the station produced a 30-minute documentary about Paul Schatz in 1973

because Paul Schatz's inversion figure was selected by this station as its (moving) signet at that time. Rudolf Steiner would certainly have been pleased, because, as he called out to his listeners in Oxford in 1922: "We have to get used to this inversion. If we don't get used to it, we will never get a proper idea of how our physical world actually relates to the spiritual world."[10] He is right, and Musil would also be pleased by this.

1 Robert Musil: *Tagebücher* (Volume 8, 1920).Published by Adolf Frisé Reinbek, 2nd edition 1983, p. 389.
2 Tobias Langscheid: *Willy A. Bachofen AG, Die Turbula – Eine wechselvolle Geschichte mit Zukunft*. In: Paul Schatz: *Rhythmusforschung und Technik*. Stuttgart, 2n edition 1998, p. 165.
3 Rudolf Steiner, lecture, June 1, 1922 in: *Anthroposophie und Naturwissenschaft.* In: *Westliche und östliche Weltgegensätzlichkeit*. GA 83, Dornach 1981, p. 18f.
4 Paul Schatz Stiftung, flyer.
5 Paul Schatz: *Betrachtungen zur Bildhauerei*. In: Matthias Mochner (Hg.): *Paul Schatz Architektur und Umstülpung*. Dornach 2013, p. 335.

6 Ibid, p. 336ff.
7 Ibid, p. 367f.
8 Lecture, Dornach, June 28, 1914. In: *Wege zu einem neuen Baustil*. GA 286, p. 76.
9 Katalog: *Rudolf Steiner – Die Alchemie des Alltags,* published by Mateo Kries, Vitra Design-Museum, Weil 2010, p. 120. See also the catalog publihsed by Markus Brüderlin and Ulrike Groos: *Rudolf Steiner und die Kunst der Gegenwart* with works by Jan Albers, Tony Cragg, Ólafur Elíasson, Helmut Federle, Katharina Grosse, Anish Kapoor and others, Dumont Verlag Cologne 2010.
10 Rudolf Steiner, Vortrag, Oxford, 22. August 1922. In: *Das Geheimnis der Trinität*. GA 214, p. 157.

"You have to invert your life!"

Panta rhei

The oloid and water

Tobias Langscheid

10

The formula "pantha rei", everything flows, attributed to the philosopher Heraclitus, best describes the oloid's shape and action. Since this solid is a figure molded by time, it "exists" only by means of a straight line, the space diagonal of the inverted cube. As a philosopher like Thales of Miletus, Heraclitus is the godfather of "flowing geometry" as Paul Schatz called the relationship of this form to water but also to air. Thus, the inner relation between the oloid and water is already given by the nature of its formation – the spatial flowing movement. If you let the oloid tumble on a table, the meandering process makes this correlation obvious.

left
Oloid used for mixing water

right
Rolling pattern of a bronze oloid on a blue pigment background

Paul Schatz divided the inversion kinematics system that he discovered into twelve different sub—applications and assigned the oloid
to the aqueous and aerial elements out of a deep inner certainty.
Both areas are related to fluid mechanics and in the course of time
it turned out that the shape of the oloid has a whole range of useful
aerodynamic and hydrodynamic properties.

One of the characteristics of the motion of inversion of the cube
is that we have a powerful left-right motion, comparable to paddling in
kayaking or the movements of the fins of fish. As the oloid is moving
in water, left—and right-turning vortices detach from the oloid circles
in an alternating pattern. For this purpose, the oloid must be attached
at two points. It may be expedient to use the two centers of the circles
that are at right angles to each other. These points can be used to
drive the two axes. At the same time, the distance of the axes defines

Just as a river makes
its way through a plain,
so does the oloid move
across a surface

Oloid

a cube edge and is part of the spatial chain gear, which moves the oloid pulsating in a loop shaped like a figure eight through space.

In water, the pulsating moving oloid generates 120 to 200 oscillations per minute with a clear direction of flow. Paul Schatz already observed this in his bathtub on a model in 1934. If the water flowing off the oloid is colored, it becomes visible how far this pulsating stream of vortices stretches. It is three-dimensional and covers the entire volume of a pond or a large basin.

It is amazing how little energy is required to completely mix a large volume. For example, an oloid agitator can homogenize a pond of 20,000 cubic meters. This is equivalent to a volume that fills an area the size of a football field at a depth of three meters. The power the oloid needs for this is insignificant at around 200 watts only. If you distribute this energy over the total volume, you get an amazingly low energy density of 0.01 watts per cubic meter. Minimal oscillating energy pulses are sufficient to activate the microbiology: The microbes

The oloid generates left and right turning vortices in the water in an alternating pattern.

Panta rhei

develop a powerful metabolic process that decomposes the biological loads of the water extremely efficiently.

Another feature of the oloid further stimulates the previously described process caused by oxygen activated in many different ways. The total surface of the water becomes activated in waves, the pond surface water begins to breathe again. A calm surface of water absorbs about 3 grams of oxygen per square meter per day, an agitated surface up to 15 grams. If we take the pond described above as an example, the water surface activated with an oloid takes up five times more oxygen than that without an oloid.

In addition, the oloid gently "inverts" the entire water volume because of its three-dimensional spreading stream of pulsing vortices. The oxygen-rich layers on the surface are moved to the layers above the sediment, which are usually poor in oxygen. That is where sediments contaminate the water. The microorganisms are supplied with water rich in oxygen by means of rhythmic currents, and the sludge, the dead biological material, is thus disintegrated.

The oloid technique described above is only the simplest of the uses envisioned by Paul Schatz. He built oloids that treat the water inside them as early as the late 1960s. The oloid mixes atmospheric oxygen and polluted water, and the tumbling motion causes intense mixing and revitalization of the liquid. The water treated this way is returned to the moving oloid, which distributes this oxygen/water mixture through-

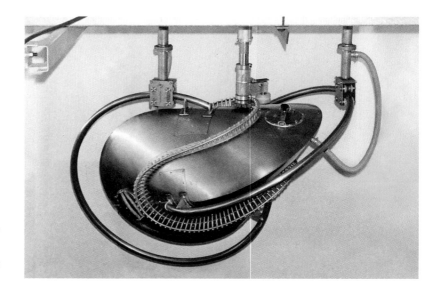

Oloid (400 liter capacity) with a rotating cone drive and a throughput for oxygen supply to clean up lakes, built by the OLOID AG for the aeration of the Niederwürzbach pond in the Saarland, 1976

Oloid

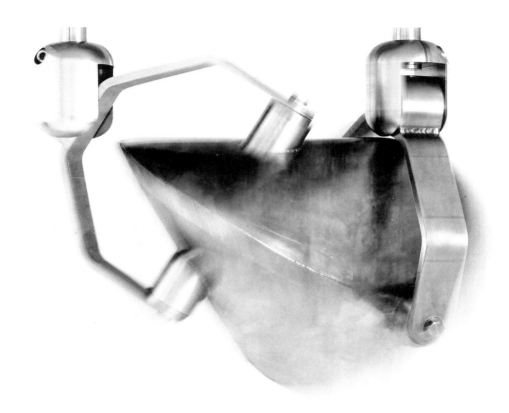

Oloid used in water
and sewerage purifica-
tion, 2018

out the lake or reservoir. In a pilot project at the Nierwürzbach reservoir in Saarland, Germany, an 800-liter oloid revitalized the 15-hectare
lake in 1976. In addition to oloids used for mixing, there are oloids
specially developed for water purification that are equipped with a
flow-through system.

Paul Schatz also developed oloids with a strainer shell. This
could be used, for example, to include plant materials that purify the
flowing water parallel to mixing it with oxygen. Finally, we should mention the possibility of constructing the oloids in a reduced form consisting of two circular discs interlocked with each other. Along with the
described gentle water treatment by the oloid, Paul Schatz recognized
the possibility of equipping ships with oloid propulsion systems. He
built the first models and a large oloid that could drive a boat. In 1938,

Two oloids for ship pro-
pulsion, 2021

for the first time, a boat was set in motion by means of oloids on the
Augster Rhine reservoir near Basel, Switzerland.

Since 2011, the Paul Schatz Foundation has been pursuing Paul
Schatz's research and technical development approach for the development of an inversion kinematic ship propulsion system in several
stages. To this end, it equipped a small catamaran with oloids and a
specially developed control system. To move a ship, two parallel drives
must always be used to compensate the vibrations caused by an oloid.

Oloid

Initial tests have clearly demonstrated the smooth flow development. The fact that the oloid shape can be modified, and also the inversion kinematics themselves, give rise to the hope that this will result in completely new ship propulsion systems. The vision of the future in which a propulsion system not only provides the ship's thrust, but at the same time also treats the water gently or even purifies it under certain circumstances, is groundbreaking for the preservation and recovery of our bodies of water.

The oloid
returns some-
thing to nature

Gerhard Heid
Beate Oberdorfer

11

Sonett has been producing ecological detergents and cleaning agents for more than 40 years. In order to perform the cultural feat of washing and cleaning, we must denature water, i.e. we must remove the tension of the water's surface so that the water does not roll off the textiles, but can penetrate them and dissolve the dirt. This principle is common to all detergents, whether conventional, or the most ecological.

At Sonett we aim to not only burden nature somewhat less with our products, but on the contrary, to return more to nature than we take from it. That's why, from the outset, we focused on the question of how we can use our products to restore vitality to nature. During our research for answers to this question, we came across Paul Schatz's oloid and the experiments of the designer Hermann Dettwiler in the 1980s and 1990s, with the oloid as a rolling and mixing body.

We conducted our own experiments with the movement of water in the oloid and were fascinated by the beautiful 8-shaped oscillation in its interior. We rolled the oloid on the ground, so the pulsating rhythm of the oloid movement got its full effect and was transferred to the liquid inside. This was exactly what we were looking for as a rhythmic movement for our balsamic detergent additives. The oloid's lemniscate is a movement inherent to water, as seen in meandering river courses, for example. This is a peculiarity of the multitude of anomalies and mysteries of water as the essence of all life.

We produce our detergent additive in our oloid, which has a capacity of about 60 liters, three times a year – at Christmas, Easter and Michaelmas. The finished product is then added in very small quantities to all our products. Our rolling oloid consists of a glass body clamped in a stainless steel frame. In terms of manufacturing technology already, this mixing device is a top achievement of sophisticated glass craftsmanship – the glass had to be melted in four parts over the blank oloid mold and then precisely joined together.

Continuous mixing oloid technique

Our detergent additive manufactured in the manner described above, which we consider to resemble the biodynamic preparations used in Demeter agriculture, gives us a unique position in the entire field of organic detergents and cleaning agents. This applies both to the product itself, but above and beyond that, to our motivation to return vitality to nature, i.e. to refine nature instead of exploiting it. This is in line with Paul Schatz's ambition expressed in 1976 about his own work: "The key motive of my research was and is to create mechanisms that do not have any destructive influence on nature."[1]

Our new raw material tank features another oloid application. While we move the balsamic additives inside the oloid, we move the

Oloid and edge cuboid

The oloid returns something to nature

oloid in the liquid itself inside this tank. The task here was to ensure continuous mixing of 40,000 liters. An oloid measuring only 40 centimeters with a power of 200 watts manages this without any problems in this large tank, surprisingly enough. On the one hand, this is a qualitative advance, but also extremely remarkable because the tank construction company had originally planned two conventional agitators with five to ten times the power for this tank size.

Over the past few years, Sonett has added two additional rhythmic techniques to the life stimulating oloid techniques: water vortexing and fluidic oscillators. We consider our applications of the oloid as well as our further rhythmic technologies to be an organic development towards more and more life-sustaining technologies and are looking forward with excitement to what will emerge as the next step of development.

Sonett's detergent additive is created in the glass oloid three times a year

1   Mochner, Schatz. 2016: p. 444.

The oloid returns something to nature

Flying future concepts

Inspiration based on inversion and the oloid

Heinrich Frontzek

12

The path from the cube to the inversion is amazing: The cube has four spatial diagonals. If two bar bodies are removed perpendicular to one of the four spatial diagonals, a spatial belt chain is left over to form the middle part. This belt chain is an invertible ring of six links, whose movement was called "inversion" by Paul Schatz.

Festo has taken this phenomenon and transferred the belt chain into an ultralight, helium-filled, floating object under the project name 'SmartInversion'. The floating link chain is composed of six identical prisms. Each of the prisms is made of carbon fiber rods, covered with a gas-tight foil.

The smart combination of extremely lightweight construction, electric drives, and control and regulation technology made it possible for the first time to create infinitely moving inversions in the air. The movement generates a pulsating drive, which most resembles the peristaltic movement of a jellyfish.

With the goal of studying this phenomenon in greater detail, Festo, together with the German Design Council, launched an interdisciplinary ideas competition for students in the fields of design and engineering. 75 students submitted their ideas, five of which received awards. The aim of the competition was for participants to explore the unusual principle of movement and find an industrial application for it.

The first prize went to the project 'HOCHDREI packaging machine'. It was submitted by three students from Magdeburg-Stendal University of Applied Sciences, Ann Julea Rajahkumar, Andreas Michel and Daniel Strohbach. The innovative 'HOCHDREI' machine packs

left
A cube – divided into the cube belt and two star bodies

right
Cube chain and two star bodies, historical model by Paul Schatz

Flying future concepts

bulk materials in three film strands simultaneously in one cycle. Second place was awarded to architecture student Matthias-Gabriel Kalfoğlou of the University of Stuttgart for his submission 'Architecture & Music – Dynamic Acoustics'. He designed an acoustic system that can be flexibly adapted to the respective spatial conditions and the demands of the musicians. The project 'InversionPROpeller' by David Boja, a product design student at the University of Design Schwäbisch Gmünd, made it to third place. David Boja developed a propeller that generates a recoil through inversion.

The oloid's first time in the air

While observing the inversion motion, Paul Schatz discovered another body, the oloid, that he named. During inversion, when a link of the cube chain is fixed in space, one of the three space diagonals, which is not directly connected to the fixed link, generates and envelops the oloid. This feature may be defined as the convex envelope of two equal-sized perpendicularly intersecting circles whose midpoints have a distance from each other equal to their radius. It is worth noting that the surface is exactly the same size as that of a sphere that has the same radius as the two circles creating the oloid. Paul Schatz experimented with flying and balloon models in oloid form as early as the 1940s. Initial tests with steerable oloids based on the

Model of an oloid balloon envelope, Paul Schatz, 1941

Oloid

Zeppelin model were initiated by the Berlin University of Applied Sciences in the years 2015 to 2017.

Paul Schatz's discovery of the oloid inspired Wilfried Stoll of Festo to commission another floating object so that the special features of the oloid could also be investigated in terms of fluid dynamics and as a propulsion system in the atmosphere. Again filled with helium, a dozen impellers (propellers contained in a housing) are active here, invisible from the outside, integrated into the floating object. Along the oloid edges, the impellers can generate propulsion in all spatial directions via fine air nozzles. The first floating oloid had its world premiere and underwent its first testing in Basel as part of the "90 Years of Inversion, 90 Years of Markthalle Basel" joint anniversary celebration in November 2019.

left
A helium-filled cube chain moves through the air thanks to pulsatory propulsion – comparable to the movements of a jellyfish in water, 2019

right
The oloid floating thanks to helium filling, 2019

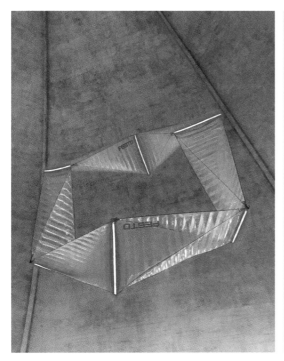

Flying future concepts

A comet in the art industry or: The UFO in the shop showcase

Andreas Chiquet

13

Although the oloid can be found in museums, it is only in their store showcases, free of function among more or less functional design gadgets. It comprises an aesthetic promise of sense that satisfies, on a primary sensorial level, even those who know neither of its origin nor of its applications, which at any rate are still not adequately implemented.

To the sculptor's eye, the shape is of striking clearness; it may be reminiscent of shells or seed forms but differs from superficially deceptively similar natural forms by virtue of the crossed edges. Even among everyday objects, the oloid has only apparent relatives. It may remind you of a wedge, but it has two fins. It rolls away on an inclined plane. But it rolls far more beautifully and "more vividly" than spheres, cones, and cylinders – whose moving appearance hardly differs from their standing one. The oloid tilts, it flutters, paddles, tumbles, shows different faces, looks back and forth while rolling, the two edges separate light and shadow in a fast play. As light as it appears, the entire surface of the body touches its path of movement, tumbling back and forth. No other body can do that. Cones and cylinders, which likewise always lie rolling on a line, are only able to do this if one disregards the flat standing surfaces and regards them as a single-surface mantle. The sphere would need infinite movement for this because it touches the ground only in one – theoretically – dimensionless point.

left
Oloids made of different types of wood, Kuboid Ltd, Basel, 2023

right
Constantin Brancusi: "Le Poisson", 1924–1926, Centre Pompidou, Paris

A comet in the art industry

If we let the oloid "roll" through the art of the 20th century in a mental game, it could be assigned to the work of the Romanian sculptor Constantin Brancusi (1876–1957) because of its exclusively convex, symmetrical and delicately stretched three-dimensionality. And one might call it the ultimate leap of quality within his life's work. For as the result of spiritual expeditions it is a concretion in contrast to the other works of the master, which as abstractions always remind one of something like fish or bird or Romanian grave stelae and thus remain attached to the "aboutness" where the American philosopher Arthur C. Danto locates art ontologically.[1]

Constantin Brancusi:
"Le Commencement
du monde", 1924–1926,
Centre Pompidou, Paris

Oloid

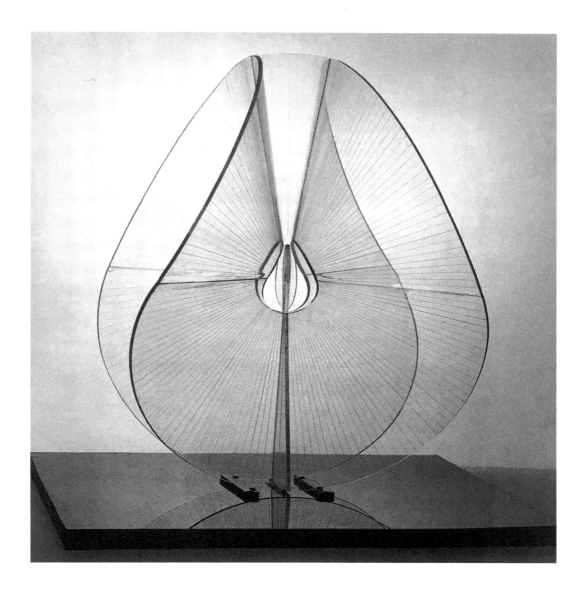

A comet in the art industry

Metal oloid at BMW
Welt Munich, 2023

Oloid

A comet in the art industry

Paul Schatz assessed the oloid not as an artistic or technical invention, but as an objective research result. But is it now, as it lies ever and ever physically in front of us, work or thing or stuff? Made of wood or stone, it is a piece of work, bent from the two-dimensional development in metal into a hollow body, becoming a vessel, as a container in the mixing device developed by Paul Schatz, it becomes stuff, in the showcase of the museum store finally an object, in the art museum it would be fine art and would probably be most appropriately placed next to Gabo's Spherical Theme (1937). Naum Gabo (1890–1977) was one of the founders of kinetic art that makes movement – usually current-induced – an integral part of its effect.[2] More modest and all the more autonomous, the oloid moves almost by itself: A slight inclination of the base sets it in motion; for its paper variant, a light breath of air is enough. In this, the oloid would be an incunabulum of cybernetic art, the nature of which is the reaction to external influences.

The oloid is a perfect example of the principles of the artistic avant-gardes of the 20th century. It dates from the time when Marcel Duchamp, faced with an airplane propeller in the 4th Salon de la Locomotion Aérienne, said to his friend Brancusi: "C'est fini la peinture, qui feramieux que cette hélice? Dis, tupeux faire ça?"[3] The abandonment of the romantic cult of genius, the dissolution of the boundary between technology and art, between civilizing and cultural aspirations, was a fundamental utopia of many avant-gardists.

Detached from the intentions of its discoverer, the oloid remains visible in public, especially in the display cases of museum stores, "Oloid. Design: Paul Schatz" is written on the price tag. In the store, it gained a right to stay esthetically, because it appears so captivating, so enchanting, so timeless. Despite Paul Schatz's efforts, the oloid has so far become less of a technical innovation and more of a hand candy, a toy, and a decorative and meditative object. It ended up in the forecourt of art – which is a mistake.

Why did the concept – compared to its potential – remain hidden for decades? What would it take to turn things around? Paul Schatz remained optimistic: "We use the wheel and the sphere as a matter of course. Why? We have been used to it for 5000 years [...] In the case of the oloid, we have only had a few decades to work with it so far. In 150 generations, we will have understood the rhythmic connection of point and circumcircle as well."

1 In ArthurC. Danto's (1924–2013) thinking art is like words or sentences. Conntrary to ordinary things it is always "aboutness."

2 First published in Kinetische Konstruktion, 1919.

3 Doïna Lemny, Brancusi & Duchamp, Paris 2000, p. 24

A comet in the art industry

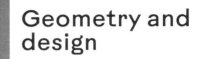

Geometry and design

Development of shape to oloid and inversion

Oliver Niewiadomski

14

The oloid is one of the younger geometric bodies. As opposed to the geometric solids known for thousands of years, such as the sphere, cube, pyramid, cylinder, etc., the oloid is still not rooted in our collective consciousness almost 100 years after its discovery by Paul Schatz. We still have not been accustomed to seeing the oloid. One reason is because we do not come across this shape frequently. For instance, we daily use cubes or cuboids stacking boxes, putting books on shelves, or handling other similar shapes, thus even those unfamiliar with these shapes become accustomed to using them. Everyone also knows and understands the sphere and circular cylinder, and they are usually easy to describe. The oloid is not easy to recognize unless you have studied it intensively.

Geometry

The oloid has no formal ancestors. It is not the derivative of anything known. Even the sphericon, often wrongly called the oloid, is similar to the oloid and has comparable properties, but it is formed from a twisted double cone and can therefore be derived from existing basic solid (Fig. p. 93).

Dealing with the geometry of the oloid, many things seem obvious. Taking a closer look, the peculiarities of its shape become more and moreobvious. Geometrically, the oloid can be developed in different ways. The cube inversion discovered by Paul Schatz is certainly the most difficult one to conceive. The definition via the main circles is more evident: The structure of the oloid is generated by two equal-sized circles intersecting at right angles, having midpoints on the periphery of each other's circles. Between the exposed, averted 2/3 of the circles,

left
The oloid – more contoured than a sphere, less angular than a polyhedron

right
The sphericon and oloid in comparison

Geometry and design

connecting lines of equal length, the "generatrices", form a one-piece, curved and unrollable surface. A surface is unrollable whenever it can become a plane. We are familiar with unrollable curved surfaces, like cones and cylinders, but also those made of plane surfaces, like cubes, cuboids and other polyhedra. (Image 02: Unrollable solid) The oloid surface's ability to unroll represents a special property in terms of its production, among other things. The structure (also of the unrolling), which is both point–and mirror-symmetrical, make it possible to cut it into identical sections, thus enabling a more efficient production. Thus, the '4shields' luminary consists of four exactly identical parts that form the oloid in combination (Fig. p. 95).

The esthetic qualities of the oloid

In addition to its special geometric properties, the oloid has special esthetic qualities that provide an extraordinary shape experience. The homogeneous solid pleases the eye and, used as a worry stone, also pleases the haptic senses. While the shape appeals to our senses, we do not immediately understand it. The oloid is not as contourless as a sphere and not as angular as a polyhedron. The oloid owes its striking appearance far from our visual habits, among other things, to its surface's constantly changing curvature, like that of a cone. In the right lighting conditions, it is especially homogeneous surfaces that give the oloid its striking appearance.

Unwindable bodies in comparison

Oloid

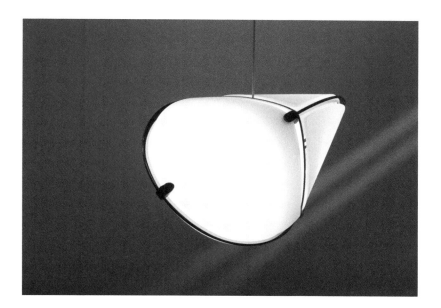

Design

Generally speaking, all design is the translation of a functional and aesthetic set of requirements into form. This form to be developed makes it possible to handle the properties and technologies of an object. During the design process, sometimes new shapes emerge that didn't exist before. In fact, the objective is to fulfill the task of finding a solution to the problem using an existing form. Basic geometric solids are the archetypes of design. There are, for instance, design products such as lamps in the form of spheres, cones, cubes and pyramids, which are familiar to all of us because we are very familiar with these basic geometric shapes. The individually developed details differentiate these designs — very much in the spirit of Charles Eames: "The details are not the details. They make the design."

Development of Design

Just as early automobiles initially looked like carriages, which they were meant to replace, and only found their own product identity with their own history; it is the role of design to give the topics related to the oloid and inversion an adequate form. Each generation has its own language and approach. In some treatments, the design concept is joined by associative issues — being adopted from foreign areas, which merge in the product. The perfect design approach, however, was described by architect Ludwig Mies van der Rohe: "Create form

Pendant lamp ‹4shields› with four identical components that complement each other to form the oloid shape, TECNOLUMEN

Geometry and design

out of the nature of the task with the means of our time."

This functional/ industrial design approach describes a design language that wants to be nothing more and nothing less than the contemporary implementation of the requirements profile, without additional adaptations. Reduced to its essentials, the margin of creative freedom becomes extremely small. Designing turns into an intellectual process. However, a product must also assert itself in the market – and ideally, beyond it. Its visual appearance is related to, and competes with, other contemporary items. This is where style and ephemeral fashion affect the design. Most of the time, however, artifacts with an extremely functional design are generally more accepted and thus last longer.

Designs for oloid and inversion

The shape of the oloid is geometrically defined, it is impossible to draft. Design is based on the idea of interpretation of the basic form. It is disassembled and reassembled, alienated, abstracted, presented in a new way, and additional elements are adjusted.

The 'ISO_PAUL' luminary cuts the oloid into isohypses and represents its form in an abstracted way by means of reference curves, similar to a ship's outline (Fig. p. 96). In the object 'TETRApaul', assigned generatrices form symmetrical tetrahedra. The oloid becomes a

left & right
Pendant luminaires
'ISO_PAUL'
and 'TETRApaul'

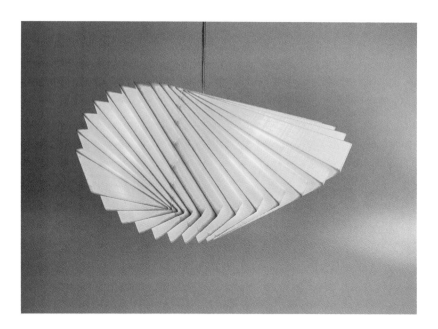

convex-concave polyhedron (Fig. p. 97). In the work 'The New Planet' by Ólafur Elíasson, the solid is deconstructed into a multitude of individual surfaces (Fig. p. 102/103). In addition, designers make use of the visual effects and appearance of colors, surface and material textures and, last but not least, the dimension: it is rather small in the case of the wooden worry stone and large in architecture such as the Heliodome.

Production and Technology

To create an oloid from a solid material, different fabrication technologies are used taking into account its geometric phenomena. Two intersecting circles can be two rings of wire, and the generatrices tensioned threads. Solid oloids are made by subtraction from solid materials such as stone or wood. Classic methods such as art casting are used as well as industrial casting, which is more precise but needs much more tooling. Other widely applied classical methods include glass and ceramic casting, which, however, require many preliminary tests to obtain accurate results according to the specified geometry (Figs. p. 99a.). Modern 3D printing processes allow the creation of stable, yet lightweight hollow bodies made of plastics without tools (Fig. p. 99a.).

The surface's capacity to unroll offers the possibility of using flat material geometries such as paper, cardboard, plastic films, sheet metal

Geometry and design

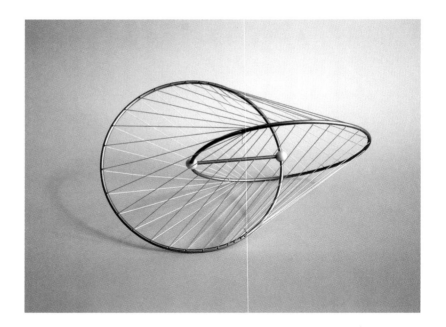

and wood veneer for the structure. In this case, the material must "follow" the changing curvature. In terms of construction, the joints between the two curved edges and the transition between the circular edges and the curved surface are difficult areas.

In the search for new manifestations, the current variety of materials with different properties always entices experimentation. The luminous object made of 3D special fabric, in combination with innovative LED lighting technology is such an attempt (Figs. p. 100).

Lamps

A common type of design objects is lamps. "A designer lamp is a sculpture that gives light, or a light source with sculptural qualities." Besides function, form and material, the magical effect of glowing is another element shaping values in this case. Thus, quite a few oloid lights were created by different designers by now, each of them embraces, in its own way, the aesthetic qualities of the oloid (Figs. p. 101).

Danish artist Ólafur Elíasson has succeeded in creating a fascinating symbiosis of unrollability and flat material. With the help of computer-generated connecting zones, he forms the oloid lit from the inside out of a flat, highly light-refracting prismatic foil, whereby its changing curvature, especially as a result of movement, leads to changing light effects (Fig. p. 101a.l.). The luminaries '4shields' use

above
Oloid figure made of two intersecting circles and tensed threads

right above
Steel molds and glass castings parts of the pendant lamp 'HALFpaul'

right below
3D printing pendant lamp 'HALFpauldruck'

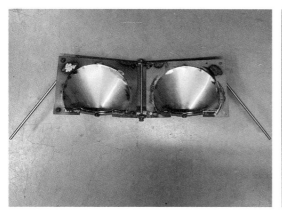

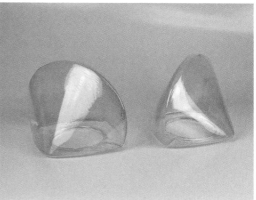

Geometry and design

unrollability together with the symmetries of the oloid to create the complete form using four identical components (Fig. p. 101 middle). Whereas the 'S_curve' luminary breaks down the unrolled parts into pairs of identical parts (Fig. p. 101 middle l.). The transparent cords of Felix Hediger's 'Filamant' luminary look like generatrices, although they are distributed in a more homogeneous way than the actual genera-trices in favor of the unity of the lampshade (Fig. p. 101a.r.). Hediger's 'FLOYD' lamps present the oloid more as a homogeneous surface, while the difficult edge seam has been elaborated as a style-defining detail (Fig. p. 101b.r.).

There are well-known esthetically sophisticated functional types, such as pendant or table lamps or the staging of the inverted cube as a kinematic light control (Fig. p. 104, 105). to elaborately staged light objects that claim the surrounding space for themselves (Fig. p. 102/103).

Paul Schatz's Design

Paul Schatz was a sculptor and technician – a combination that is very close to the designer profession. Paul Schatz's early prototypes were created entirely by hand, based on his skills. They were not in-tended to be more than the physical manifestation of his theoretical

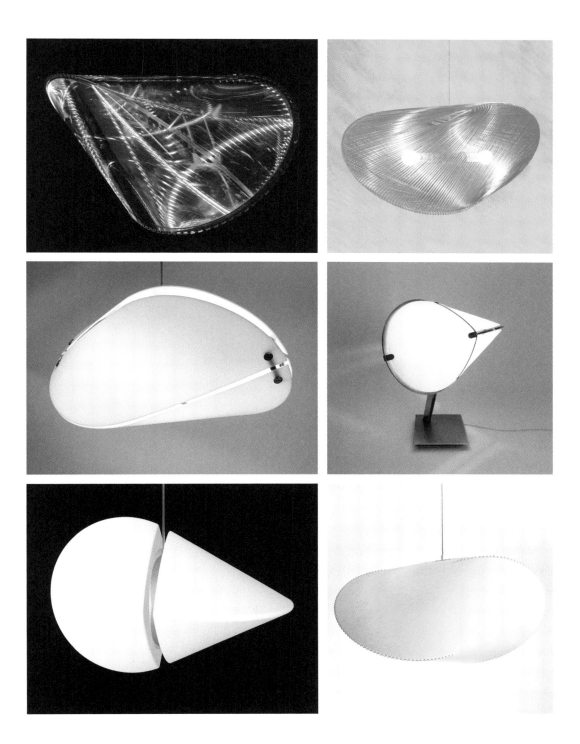

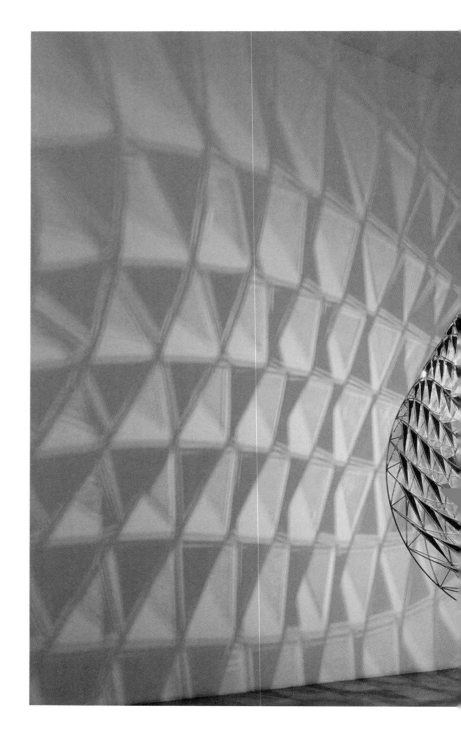

Ólafur Elíasson,
"The new planet", 2014

Oloid

Geometry and design

insights. They are working models that radiate their own charm through their — if I may say so — sometimes clumsy production: "quick and beautiful", instead of "quick and dirty." At the same time, his sculptural talent hardly came to play, as if he didn't have any additional design aspirations. That he was capable of developing a constructive-functional design product is proven by a small plastic table lamp that is a perfect industrial product. Schatz' concept shows a novel movement of the lampshade, which, however, is neither formally nor constructively related to oloid and inversion (Fig. p. 105).

Mixing vessel

Inversion and rhythm generation not only involve motion brought into form, but also the vessel necessary to do so. The design of an ideal mixing vessel follows different parameters. It should have both optimal shape for mixing and handling, which guarantees not only the best mixing result, but also offers the best conditions for filling, emptying, and cleaning. This form development process also requires several trials to

Table lamp designed by Paul Schatz with an illustration of the patent specification and preliminary sketches, 1950

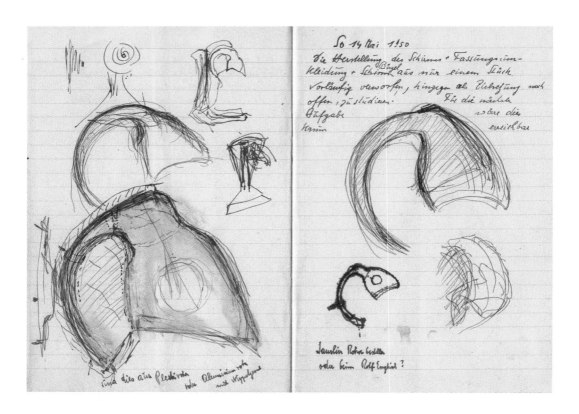

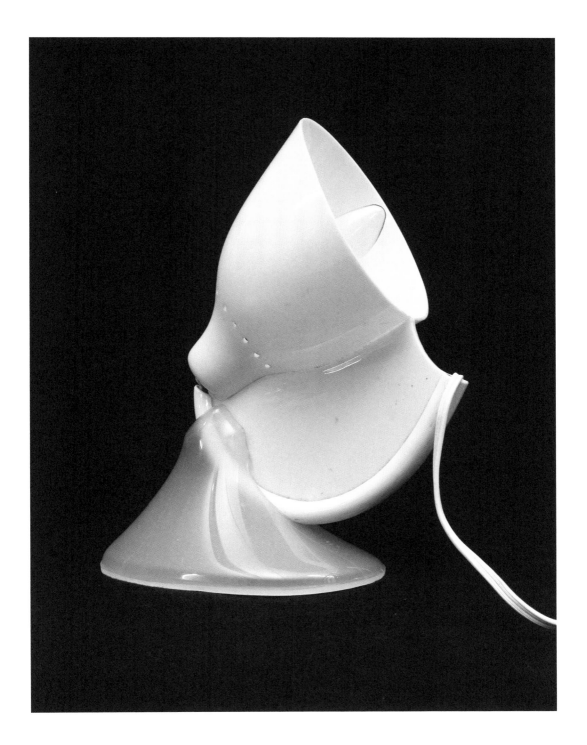

105   Geometry and design

verify the developed design. From the 3D cardboard grip model to the custom-made laboratory glass, which resulted in the "most beautiful" mixing pattern so far. The designed "handle waist" forms a shape in the section, similar to the lying lemniscate, a looping geometric curve in the shape of a prostrated figure eight, the sign of infinity.

Logic that took shape

"A picture is worth a thousand words. A model says more than a thousand pictures." The phenomena of a geometric context can be explained and "grasped" much more vividly through examples than through text and pictures. Geometric objects and shapes have their own esthetics. We find these in teaching models and objects. Design, then, refers not only to the development of utility objects, but also to the representation of geometry for its own sake, almost as in sculpture.

Steel oloid at Chateâu
Champlitte (France),
2022

Geometry and design

From form to space

The oloid in architecture

Tilo Richter

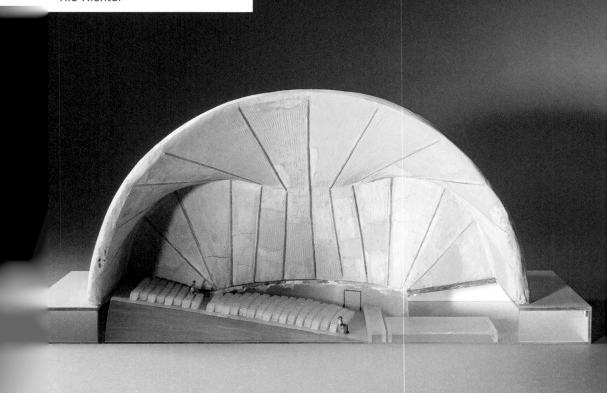

15

The history of architecture of Modernism does not suffer from a lack of search for newly shaped spaces that break with historic precedents as much as possible. Paul Schatz was deeply interested in the work of Rudolf Steiner, especially his buildings of the First and Second Goetheanum in Dornach, inaugurated in 1920 and 1928 respectively. Schatz's interest in progressive trends in architecture and sculpture made him create his own architectural designs in the 1950s, based on the principle of inversion. In the 1960s, he developed the cuboids, derived from the cube inversion. In 1968, Schatz designed a floating cultural center for Lake Zurich based on this fundamental form – which, like the oloid, evolved from motion – and was also called the Umstülpungshalle (Inverted Hall), but it was never realized. Walter Keller, also from Dornach, submitted a biomorphically shaped wave body to the same competition, which – like Schatz's – resembles sculptural works. "These are kinetic designs, which on the one hand are subject to a strict order, but which nevertheless, in association with creative imagination, take us into the endless realms of sculptural design."[1]

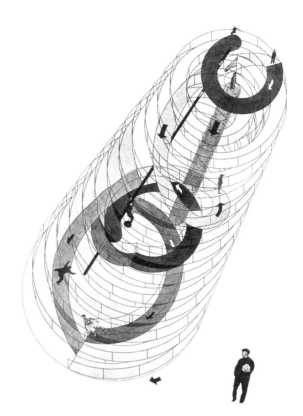

left
Paul Schatz's model of the Floating Cultural Center on Lake Zurich, 1968

right
"kinetic constructive system", László Moholy-Nagy, constructed by Stefan Sebök, 1928

From form to space

Among the important architectural studies published at the Bauhaus is the 'kinetic constructive system' conceived by Laszló Moholy-Nagy, published in 1929 in 'Bauhausbücher 14: vom material zu architektur'. Again, form emerges from motion in space. The linear forces' axes define the edges of the space, forming the volume of the building on a time level. Paul Schatz was probably not only familiar with this strongly three-dimensional design method, which was influenced by sculpture, but it probably influenced his work for many years.

Such new types of spatial forms also attracted particular interest because people were curious about the acoustic effects linked to them. A highlight of this linking of spatial and auditory experience was the Philips Pavilion by Iannis Xenakis and Le Corbusier, which was exhib-

Construction site of the Philips Pavilion for the Brussels World's Fair, Iannis Xenakis and Le Corbusier, 1958

Oloid

below
Model in cardboard by
Paul Schatz for a build-
ing on a circular floor
plan, around 1960

pp. 112–113
La Maison Solaire
'Heliodome', designed
and implemented by
Éric Wasser, Cosswiller,
2008

ited at the 1958 World's Fair in Brussels. Nine hyperbolic paraboloids
formed an impressive structure in which Edgar Varése's sound installation 'Poème électronique' could be heard during the exhibition. For
Le Corbusier, as for Paul Schatz, a construction following complicated
mathematical functions replaced conventional design. The volumes
created this way offered not only geometries previously unknown in architecture, but also a fundamentally new perception and use of space.

A prototype of the architectural oloid form is the La Maison
Solaire 'Heliodome' by Éric Wasser, built in 2008 in Cosswiller, Alsace,
France. Its shape manifests the sun's annual and diurnal cycle; basi-
cally, it is a three-dimensional sundial. With its south-facing glass
façade, which resembles a fan, and mostly closed wooden façades in
the north, the building makes use of nature and is at the same time
its geometric image. While on hot summer days the sunlight cannot
shine directly into the house, the rays of the low winter sun warm the
interior of the 'Heliodome'. Similarly, a smaller solar house designed

From form to space

by Herbert Lötscher has been located in the Valais mountain village of Erschmatt, Switzerland, at an altitude of 1250 meters since 2013.

A spectacular example of the presence of the oloid form in the history of architecture is the 2011 proposal for the extension of the Berlin Philharmonic Hall by Studio Other Spaces, founded by Ólafur Elíasson and Sebastian Behmann. In the immediate vicinity of Hans Scharoun's Philharmonie (1963) and Ludwig Mies van der Rohe's National Gallery (1968), two glass buildings are created, shaped as oloids. The upright structures, which are partly sunk into the ground, are obviously not conceived as images of the sun's course, but as symbolic volumes that enter into an exciting dialogue with the concave and tent-like forms of the Philharmonie's concert hall.

Zaha Hadid likewise redefined geometry in architecture and pushed technological boundaries with her designs. In 2013, she completed the Heydar Aliyev Center in the Azerbaijani capital of Baku, where she created a continuum of forms that flowed inside and out. The meandering motif also reappears here in an adapted and dynamic form. The intricate forms of the Changsha Meixihu International Culture & Arts Center in China, inaugurated in 2017/19, recall the movement studies Paul Schatz made based on his three-dimensional models of five-limbed systems. Likewise, affinities are evident in the 'House of the Future' planned by Georg Düx for the neighborhood of

Proposal for an extension of the Berlin Philharmonic Hall, model: Studio Other Spaces, Ólafur Elíasson and Sebastian Behmann, 2011

the Goetheanum, which would have housed the Rudolf Steiner Archive. The basis of the designs for this new contemporary building was the movement of its visitors, which would have been reflected in the architectural shapes.

"Human beings will transverse the building in sync with the shape, while their vitality makes the room regain its motion."

In the summer of 2021, the Paul Schatz Foundation developed an inverted pavilion in the form of a halved cuboid to be used for exhibition purposes in collaboration with the experimonde Wien association. In this design the half-cuboid incorporates Schatz's draft for the floating cultural

above
Zaha Hadid's Heydar Aliyev Center in Baku (Azerbaijan), 2013

pp. 116—117
Changsha Meixihu International Culture & Arts Center in Changsha (China), Zaha Hadid Architects, 2019

1   Paul Schatz: "Die Polysomatische Plastik. Zur Grundlegung neuer stereometrischer Gebilde", in: Das Werk, Architektur und Kunst, Vol. 56, 1/1969, p. 6.

2   Paul Schatz Stiftung (Ed.): Paul Schatz. Die Welt ist umstülpbar. Rhythmusforschung und Technik. Niggli Verlag Sulgen/Zurich 2008, p. 127.

Oloid

From form to space

left above
This plasticine body represents the three-dimensional form of a five-pronged inversion, Paul Schatz, 1970s

right above
Floating Cultural Center on Lake Zurich, collage by Paul Schatz, 1968

below
Draft design of an inversion-shaped chapel, around 1968

Inversion pavilion and oloid at Skulpturhalle Basel, 2022, constructed by experimonde, Vienna, shown as part of Architekturwoche Basel, 2022

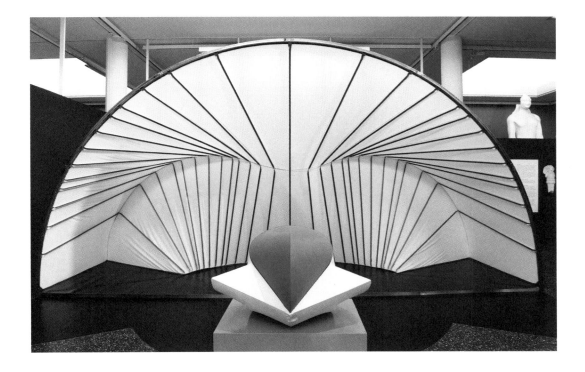

From form to space

Performing future

The future principle is the principle of movement

Vera Koppehel

16

*"Want the change. Be inspired by the flame
where everything shines as it disappears.
The artist, when sketching, loves nothing so much
as the curve of the body as it turns away."*[1]

To build an oloid is as simple as can be: Move two beer coasters together, twisted by 90 degrees to each other, up to the respective central points of the circular surfaces, and voilà – you get the tumbling basic structure of the body, which has a completely new, even revolutionary quality of motion that broadens the way we see the world.

This begs the question how come mankind didn't come up with this form of movement earlier? After all, it's easy to discover new territory. Yes, theoretically it is. But as early as 1492, Christopher Columbus made the point with his famous egg challenge – that it's not a matter of being able to do something theoretically, but of actually doing it. Whether he struck the egg lightly at the tip or simply placed it upright in salt is of no importance in this context. What is important is that he changed the way he thought and thus showed how new continents can be discovered by leaving old worlds behind. Paul Schatz did not just change his way of thinking, but, as it were, inverted it. He brought solid bodies, in this precise case a cube, into motion, i.e. into time and thus into a process of development. Out of observing and actively following

Still from: video RAUM-FILTER_INVERSION 3:1, installation with moving image and eurythmy, Vera Koppehel, 2014

Performing future

this complex geometric process, the oloid was born as a new spatial
form, as it were, out of time. In this case, the answer to the question of
'chicken or egg' is:

In the beginning was motion

And motion is also what keeps the oloid together at its core, it is
its element, its temperament. It does not want to and cannot stand
still, it wants to move and set everything around it in motion. Preferably
in the water, but also in the air. Watching Festo's 'Smart inversions' –
helium-filled floating objects in the form of an inverted cube belt and
an oloid – dance through the air with rhythmic pulsation, images of
future ships, wind turbines and ventilators come to mind.

Why actually? Creating space as a result of time is one thing. To
develop rhythmically pulsating objects from it, which fulfill a function,
is something else. This additionally requires the ability of inversion: to
develop our ability to guide our thoughts and to feel the form into the
surroundings, into the periphery. Because an exploration of the principle of inversion, which is defined quite dramatically by the fourfold
passage through infinity and crossing point zero, the nothingness, needs
courage. Since the center of our contemplative awareness sometimes
shifts inside and sometimes outside, stretches to the point, concen-
trates on space, and challenges a kind of interdisciplinary exploration

Oloid

of external interiors as well as internal exteriors. The oloidal behavior becomes an interactive performing event for form structures of the invisible on the inner stage and this is the connection, the interface to art, to moving art.

To be performing eurythmically active means to me to be able to be more and more at home in the center as well as in the periphery and to playfully deal with the laws of "inside out / outside in". I, or rather what is inside me, dance in improvisation of dynamic sequences between wakefulness and dream and the fragile states of consciousness in between. I walk the tightrope of everyday life, along the unstable balance between the past and the future, exploring what we call the present moment where something new, really new, can emerge. This crucial moment occurs in situ during the dance connecting breath and exhalation, at turnarounds, at leaps and bounds, at turning points.

It is on these transition areas from word to silence, from sound to color or from silence to action that I try to transfer aspects of the idea of inversion into something concrete, to something visible, audible and comprehensible.[2]

Performance Vera Koppehel, Fondation Beyeler, 2016, in the background the painting by Franz Marc «Die Wölfe (Balkankrieg) (The wolves – Balkan war)» of the year 1913

Performing future

Inversion star according
to Paul Schatz, 1962,
progressive movement
of six cube edges during
an inversion

124   Oloid

Performing future

Organic interactions

"The principle of synthesis, the interrelation and interaction of word and sound, sound and color, sound and gesture, and finally the organic interaction of the arts (and not their mechanical unification), the natural, the unforced transition from the pure language of one art to the language of another – all these are primary concerns of our time, as it passes under the sign of the 20th century."[3]

Paul Schatz elicited this third quality of motion, the inversion motion, or rather managed to extract it out of the threshold between art and science in 1929. This birth wasn't an easy one. For what if the universe not only rotates, spins, stretches and spirals, but also turns itself upside down and inside out? And what if we can recognize this intuitively, because we have carried it out ourselves with our birth as a big dance from the narrowness of the cosmos into the widths of the mother's belly? This is because the human body has all three spatial planes – sagittal, horizontal and vertical – and our spine and hip movements combine all three spatial directions in harmony as we move lemniscally.

We can experience this as Copernican imposition of the 3rd millennium, but the principle of motion is the principle of the future. After the physical laws, mankind is now discovering and conquering more and more laws of the living, of nature. Wanting to understand and apply inversion is an opportune challenge for mankind in the 21st century.

1 Rainer Maria Rilke.*The Sonnets to Orpheus.*Second Part, XII. Sonnet.
2 See *Umstülpung bewegt** homage to paul schatz 2016 as well as RAUMFILTER_INVERSION_3:1

Installation with motion picture and eurythmics. 2014:www.arte-vera.com/buehne.
3 Arthur Lourié (1891–1966) composer. First published in Strelec, St. Petersburg 1915.

Acknowledgements

The editors of this publication, the Paul Schatz Foundation and the Paul Schatz Society, would like to thank the following institutions and companies for their generous financial support:

BŒENICKE

lustenberger
+partners

Obermark

FESTO

FONDATION
GOLDAPFEL

SWISS HEALTH ALLIANCE
DIPLOMATIC CORPS SONDERMISSION

SWISSLOS
*Fonds des
Kantons Solothurn*

JULEN GROUP

TECNOLUMEN®

KUBOID
INVEST AG

REDEFINING BANKING

Imprint

A publication of the Paul Schatz Foundation and the Paul Schatz Society

The Deutsche Nationalbibliothek lists this publication in the Deutsche Nationalbibliografie; detailed bibliographic data are available on the Internet at http://dnb.dnb.de

ISBN 978-3-7212-1025-5

© 2024 Niggli, imprint of Braun Publishing AG, Salenstein
www.niggli.ch

1st edition 2024

Editors: Tobias Langscheid, Tilo Richter
Translation: Sandra Ellegiers, Cosima Talhouni
Editing: Cosima Talhouni
Graphic concept and layout: Benjamin Wolbergs
Proofreading: Sandra Ellegiers